THE MONTESSORI ALZHEIMER'S PROJECT

Applying Montessori Insights to Dementia Care

Lyle Weinstein
Greg MacDonald

1st edition

Copyright © 2018 Lyle Weinstein

All rights reserved

ISBN: 978-1-9995194-0-7

BISAC: Health & Fitness/Diseases/Alzheimer's & Dementia

The Montessori Alzheimer's Project

Dedication

To my parents,
whose journey together became a continuous display of warmth.

To Maria Montessori,
whose insights into human development continue to transform lives of the young, the old, and everyone in between.

And, as always, to the more than 5 million Alzheimer's patients in the United States and the many millions elsewhere,
now and in the future, who can only benefit from the kindness of genuine caregiving.

The Montessori Alzheimer's Project

Preface

One of the truly extraordinary aspects of dealing with dementia in a loved one is the kindness and warmth that is generated among caregivers. I was the beneficiary of this during my father's illness. The patience within the caregiver community is suffused with warmth, which is triggered the moment someone speaks to another caregiver about their own family's journey with dementia.

Medical research into the causes of dementia and potential treatments is critical for the future. But, for those afflicted now, and their caregivers, I believe that the impact of Montessori insights to human development will be of far more immediate benefit to those in need right now.

Montessori is an educational method based on observing how people engage their world during the different stages of human development. This a companion piece to *The Alzheimer's Family Manual.* It is an extension of those lessons into the Montessori framework.

Let us continue to educate each other, to support each other, and to be the kind, stable, and critically important reference points needed by those afflicted with dementia.

The Montessori Alzheimer's Project

Table of Contents

Dedication……………..………………………………………5

Preface ………………...……………………………...………7

Introducing the Montessori Alzheimer's Project…………..11

Chapter 1 Montessori and Dementia Care………………15

Chapter 2 The Importance of Observation………….……21

Chapter 3 Expanding Supportive Environment: Speech…37

Chapter 4 Preparing the Environment: The Kitchen……..51

Chapter 5 The Prepared Environment for Meals…………65

Chapter 6 Applied Journaling……………………………77

Chapter 7 The Supportive Environment in Toileting…….91

Chapter 8 Cuing and Redirection………………...………107

Chapter 9 Cuing for Visitors……………………………119

Chapter 10 Caring for the Caregiver……………………129

Afterword……………………………………………….143

The Montessori Alzheimer's Project

Introducing the Montessori Alzheimer's Project (MAP)

Once there was a rhythm to life that was familiar. It was comfortable and made sense from one day to the next. It was an agreed upon rhythm that was maintained by every family member through the ups and downs of life. And then, the rhythm was disturbed. It stopped working so predictably.

At first, the disturbance was intermittent. Then, it started happening more often. At a certain point, a doctor made a diagnosis, using words like dementia or Alzheimer's Disease. Sometimes the doctor simply suggested that there was some memory loss.

As the impact of this condition became more noticeable, life became less comfortable. Days and often nights became less ordinary. Predictable rhythms could no longer be counted on in quite the same way.

This happened in my family when my father was diagnosed with Alzheimer's Disease at around the age of 54. The changes that had been happening in my father and our family interactions were suddenly clarified in that explanation. Our world changed. At a particularly difficult moment in our family's journey, I wrote down what I might say to someone who was just beginning their own version of that journey. That writing first became an audiotape program to support caregivers, and then part of my book, *The Alzheimer's Family Manual*.

Decades later, as friends and acquaintances contacted me about dementia in their aging parents. I considered again what I might say to anyone at the beginning of, or even deep into, that journey. The information in *The Alzheimer's Family Manual* remained relevant, at least to the people to whom I passed on the material. In the meantime, I encountered Montessori education, first as practiced by my wife, Riza Weinstein, in the school community she founded, and then as understood and taught by Greg MacDonald. This led me to consider with them how we might benefit individuals with dementia as well as their caregivers.

It is clear that there is a path to provide such benefit, a path of kindness and sanity. It is a path that can be traveled by individuals with dementia and their caregivers. That is the genesis of the Montessori Alzheimer's Project.

I invite you to walk with me along that path. Together, we can enhance the quality of life for the individual with dementia as well as for the caregiver. It is a method to reclaim some stability and ease in many of the ordinary rhythms of life together.

I have used the phrase "individual with dementia" to refer to people with the various forms of dementia that all need care. While dementia appears in both men and women, I have used the male pronoun in this book where pronouns were necessary. I have done this for readability, as well as in remembrance of my father.

Our goal is to help transform many of the difficulties of dementia and dementia care. It is to engender solutions and

The Montessori Alzheimer's Project to empower caregivers dealing with their new reality of life with dementia.

The Montessori Alzheimer's Project

Chapter 1 - Montessori and Dementia Care

Most people are aware of Montessori education as a method of teaching children, particularly young children. We know that an individual with dementia is not a child. What does an educational model primarily associated with preschool, and to lesser extents infant/toddler development as well as elementary and adolescent schools, have to offer to those with dementia and their caregivers? In short, what is it about the theory and practice of Montessori education that makes it relevant to dementia care?

Let's be clear at the very outset that the Montessori Alzheimer's Project (MAP) does not view individuals with dementia as children. Individuals suffering from Alzheimer's and other forms of dementia are adults, not children. We begin with this understanding clearly in place.

MAP applies key insights common to all Montessori education to the specific practical needs of those with dementia, and to their caregivers. These include the using the foundations of the Montessori Method beginning with Observation, then the 3 S's of Standardize, Simplify and Signage, and finally, Redirection. The application of these foundational insights will be explained and highlighted throughout the material presented in this book.

But first, let's discuss the impact of dementia and what Montessori has to offer as both a theory and practice for caregivers.

Abilities and Capacities Change

We know from the work of Maria Montessori, and of many other experts in the field of child development, that the mental capacities of children are not static. These capacities change as children develop and mature. Each change is instrumental in moving the individual forward along a developmental path that begins even before infancy. We usually consider the development to have reached completion when the individual becomes an adult.

However, the capacities of an adult with dementia are not static. They change as the disease progresses. While a child's developmental path brings increasing ease and abilities for relating with life's tasks, the changes in adults with dementia result in reducing ease and greater difficulties relating to life's tasks.

That being said, Montessori can be summarized briefly by the question, *"How can we best support someone whose capacities are constantly changing?"*

This question applies to both developing children and to adults with dementia. In fact, it is a question relevant to all stages of life. Keeping that view in mind, we can find many profound insights in Montessori applicable to the diverse issues that come along with the onset and progression of dementia in adults.

The Montessori Alzheimer's Project

The Importance of Observation

To properly consider the application of Montessori to dementia care, we begin with Dr. Montessori's original approach, using one of the fundamental principles of the Montessori method: Observation.

Dr. Montessori developed her approach to educating children based on closely observing their interactions with the world. Observation means seeing how they perceive and experience the world. Based on her ongoing Observation, she began to create an environment that supported their existing intellectual and physical capacities while, at the same time, encouraging the development of those capacities. In other words, the environment established reference points for the children that they did not yet have the capacity to establish for themselves.

What might dementia caregivers take from this approach?

First, by carefully and systematically observing individuals with dementia, we can detect important patterns. These patterns change as the illness progresses. Some may disappear, new ones may arise. This is true with respect to both their interpersonal and their environmental interactions. These changing patterns are clues to help us understand what need the individual with dementia is expressing in real time.

Second, we can observe our own reactions as we care for a loved one afflicted with dementia. Third, we can observe the interactions among family members dealing with the progressively demanding impact of the dementia.

Observation conducted in this manner is fundamental to the Montessori Alzheimer's Project approach. It is the keystone for every caregiver who wishes to provide the best care for their loved one, for themselves, and for their family.

As you explore this book, and perhaps more in-depth MAP training, you may find that your power of Observation develops in a way that refines its focus on the effects of dementia. With that strengthening power of Observation, you will be able to respond with ever increasing confidence to the many demands of caring for the individual with dementia. You will be able to respond ever more effectively.

Observation with the MAP approach will prepare you to enhance the stable, patient, and kind day-to-day care needed for your loved one. It takes time to develop these skills and your confidence in them. But, as you begin to read the messages found in your Observations, you will know which response is likely the best one available to you at the time. Not every response will work as you hope, but every response will help with your identification of the needs the individual with dementia is showing you. And that will lead to refining your future responses aimed at addressing that need.

Importance of Cues

As you work with MAP principles, you will become aware of a recurring theme for environmental support: *Cues.*

The Montessori Alzheimer's Project

We all function within our day-to-day life using cues. We read cues in the environment, and we put cues out into the environment. One of the most powerful ways to support someone who has dementia is to provide them with cues that they can understand.

As the abilities they've relied upon in the past for daily life activities begin to erode, providing appropriate cues can allow for continued safe engagement with the world. We can engage their then-available capacities by providing cues that can be relied upon as needed.

Providing appropriate cues allows for a greater opportunity to live one's life safely within the context of dementia. It allows caregivers to extend that safety for as long as possible. These are the goals.

Cues allow for independence with support as needed. Self-esteem and connection are preserved. As a result, the individual with dementia can participate in daily life with less stress. That's good for everyone; the individual with dementia and the caregivers.

Notes

Chapter 2 - The Importance of Observation

When we observe individuals with dementia, we are not looking at them as if they were laboratory specimens under a microscope. It is quite the opposite. Observation here means looking at them with insight and empathy. It is seeing how they interact with and within their personal environment.

Here is a basic framework of questions for beginning Observations of individuals with dementia:

- How have they and those interactions changed?
- How have they remained the same?
- What skills do they access easily?
- What skills seem to be disappearing?
- What skills seem to have disappeared?
- What seems to upset them?
- What puts them at ease?

Observing a Greeting

Here is a practical example of Observation in action and the information you might gain from it. When someone greets an individual who they know has dementia, possibly their parent, the greeting might be, *"Hi Dad, good to see you again. Do you remember who I am?"* Observe what happens next.

From personal experience, I can tell you that the likely reaction of the individual with dementia will indicate an increased level of tension in both their body and their demeanor. Why might that be the case? It is because they experience the interaction as a test. And they know that it is a test they might fail.

Observe what happens when they answer. If they answer correctly, the body language shifts to signaling a relaxation of much of the tension, but not of all of it. Why doesn't all the tension dissolve? It is likely that they are worried that there might be more questions coming. It reflects a fear of more tests. There might be more questioning that may end in failure next time.

If they answer incorrectly, you will see a far more intense reaction to the perceived test. Their body language may express anger, as may their words. Alternatively, it may signify withdrawal and silence. Sometimes, it can trigger a catastrophic reaction of full-blown panic because the dementia's impact is now being exposed.

Observing the Questioner

The reason we want to observe is to gather useful information in order to develop appropriate cuing. Keep that in mind. As we continue the Observation, focus now on the person asking the question because there is more data to be collected.

When the individual with dementia's demeanor changes, whatever change that may be, it impacts the questioner. The impact will show up immediately in the body language of the questioner. Usually, it mirrors the changes in tension and demeanor of the person questioned.

If the answer is forthcoming and correct, the body language of the questioner indicates a relaxation of tension. This telegraphs to the individual with dementia that they have passed the test. Unfortunately, it simultaneously confirms that the question was indeed a test – and that the questioner was clearly aware the answer given might be wrong.

If the answer is wrong, or perhaps is given only after a bit too much time has elapsed, the body language of the questioner communicates that the individual with dementia has exposed that they are even more ill than they knew. They have failed this test.

Imagine the pressure that this puts on someone with dementia.

Avoid Testing

To experience interpersonal communication as an ongoing test is incredibly frightening. Consider how you would feel if every encounter with someone – including your most precious loved ones – was a test, and if that test was an assessment of your mental condition, with a judgment being made on the spot.

For individuals suffering from dementia, this realization can generate anger as well as fear, often at the same time. They resist being continually tested, and being continually stressed in each interaction. This is true whether or not the questioner appreciates that their question is being experienced as a test. Unfortunately, the encounter is usually and correctly assessed by the individual with dementia as a test.

Typically, the questions are asked because the questioners are concerned about their loved one. They want to gauge the progress of the dementia. The questions are coming out love. But, it is not just coming from the affection they feel for the individual with dementia.

Just as important as their wish to give affection, the questioner usually is seeking assurance that their connection to the individual with dementia remains intact in some way that comforts the questioner. They hope to get that assurance by hearing the correct answer to the basic question.

The answer they want is the subtext of the question. It is, "Does she still remember me? Does she still love me in the same way? Does she still know I'm her son?" The tone and body language of the questioner always conveys that subtextual concern.

For the individual with dementia who is focusing on the less conceptual but more easily understood body language, these foundations for the concern are no longer intuited or understood. All that comes through from the questioner is the concern, the worry, and the potential judgment. The message received by individuals with dementia is that they may fail, will fail, or have failed in some way that they may or may not understand.

This brings up another Montessori principle: Applied Humility. It guides one to focus on the needs of the individual to be educated, rather than upon yourself and your needs as the teacher. For caregivers, the application of this kind of focus is critical to working with an individual with dementia. And in this scenario of greetings, the subtext of those questions is not a need of the individual with dementia. They are expressing a need of the questioner.

The Prepared Environment

Ongoing Observation can provide us with tremendous guidance in applying Montessori insights. It is the power of applied Observation that gives us early warnings of the need for additional or varying levels of support. And it is our task to adjust our conduct and the environment to the appropriate level of support.

We have made the necessary Observations. Now we look next to establishing a "prepared environment" for supporting the individual with dementia. The creation of prepared environments is another key Montessori principle to which we will return again and again. It is an incredibly powerful tool with benefits for adults with dementia as well as for their caregivers.

The environment we have been discussing here is interpersonal communications. It involves a verbal exchange in the context of a greeting. That environment includes words, but is not limited to them. The content is delivered with particular vocal tones and body language that communicate more than just words.

Our goal is to organize the environment so as to maximize the opportunity for a positive interchange. In other words, it is to set up the foundation for having a successful greeting that your loved one will experience as filled with warmth. We want a communication in which he will be at ease. To do this, we must prepare an environment that minimizes the stress and eliminates any elements of a test.

Confidence

First, applying humility eliminates the focus on ourselves. Rather, we remain focused on the needs of the individual with dementia.

Next, continuing in the context of a greeting, it is important to have confidence and to project that confidence. But, what confidence? It is confidence that the relationship you have to the individual with dementia exists independent of their illness. It is not based on their recollection of your name, or even your face. It is not based on whether or not they know you are their spouse, their child, or their oldest friend.

It is confidence in the heart connection you have to the individual with dementia. That is what needs to be expressed on the spot; in words, vocal tone and body language. This confidence is extended to the individual with dementia based upon what you put out to them as you speak your first words of greeting.

Testing attempts to gather information from someone. It is a kind of taking rather than giving. A loving relationship is one of giving, not taking. So, focus on the giving. Humility and confidence enable us to focus on the needs of the individual with dementia rather than on any needs or desires that we might have.

The goal is to put the individual with dementia at ease. At that moment, our own hopes and fears are not relevant. Set them aside until you are in a place and at a time where you can focus on your own needs. This is something you need to do, as we discuss in Chapter 10, but you need to do it away from the individual with dementia.

Montessori method focuses on giving information, rather than upon a question and answer approach. With children, questions only come when the Montessori teacher is confident that the child will be able to successfully provide an answer. Before that time, Montessori teachers demonstrate what is to be done. They tell the children just enough to engage their attention. They lead the child to the answer. There is no criticism as to when or whether a correct answer to a question will come. The focus remains on the developmental needs of the child. This same approach provides guidance and benefit in caregiving.

It is quite easy to eliminate the testing element from a greeting when you focus on giving. This involves changing our habits. As adult caregivers, we have the capacity to intentionally change them. Consider that our adult interactive habits are predicated on the expectation of the other person's ability to respond. Now understand that these expectations need to be adjusted in light of the dementia.

Adapt this Montessori approach to the needs of an adult with dementia in the context of a greeting. Simply greet them with something like: *"Hi Dad, so good to see you again. I'm your son, Lyle."*

Breaking down this greeting, you see that you have offered them easily accessible bits of information. You said first that it was good to see them; second, "again" lets them know that you'd seen them before; third, you identified your relationship to them; and fourth, you provided your name. All these bits of reference points that they need are provided without requiring any answer from them.

Framing the greeting in this way puts the individual with dementia at ease. There is no questioning involved – neither conceptual nor of the relationship. It gives them what they need to engage with you. Therefore, there is no test. There is no foreshadowing of future testing. That means you have included another cue of safety for them.

With everyone at ease, you open the gateways to ongoing positive interactions – based on connection rather than testing. Transitions can be a stumbling block. Supporting that greeting process enables the transition to be completed safely, without tension. Now, you can engage in a chat, go for a walk, have a cup of tea, and so forth. In short, we are using the Montessori concept of a prepared environment to support the connection, not to prove or disprove it.

The Montessori Alzheimer's Project

So, to summarize communicating without testing:

- We began by observing the individual with dementia.
- We continue by observing our own participation in the interchange.
- We take the Observations and modify the environment of the interaction to support the individual dementia.
- We extend warmth uncompromised by our own wishes.

Extend this understanding of the greeting environment into other interpersonal contexts. No one feels comfortable when someone who clearly seems to know us approaches us, and we simply cannot remember their name. We usually experience embarrassment. We likely feel that we have made a mistake, we have failed the test. This is exactly the experience from which we want to protect the much more vulnerable individual with dementia.

Name Tags

Consider how we can prepare the environment to eliminate this difficulty of not remembering the name of someone greeting us, or our relationship with them. Think about situations involving people without dementia who might need cues for names. Here is a very clear example of how Signage can be an unobtrusive but key support in the home.

At conferences, attendees are almost always given name tags. Name tags are provided to enhance interactions among a group whose members are not familiar. Everyone who attends conferences understands this use of name tags. It is a simple device that supports comfortable interactions with new faces. If you are introduced to someone at the coffee table before the conference formally starts, it is unlikely you will remember their name. With the name tag, there is no problem. How might this apply to individuals with dementia?

We know that the ability to read is not affected in lock-step with the ability to remember. Memory erodes more quickly than the ability to read. Even if an individual is unable to recall the name of a person, they may still be able to read, pronounce, and understand their name. Especially in early stages of dementia, simply having people wearing name tags in the environment can be a boon to those with dementia.

In the home, having name tags for visitors makes things much easier. It quietly eliminates some of the testing atmosphere that happens when someone visiting initiates a greeting. With name tags, family members and friends who are not familiar with the MAP approach to greetings will be less likely to ask testing questions in their greetings. It just doesn't make sense to ask, *"Who am I?"* when you're already labeled with that information. And if there is any hesitation, you can simply point to the name tag and read it for the individual with dementia, which provides another level of support built upon the name tag.

Depending on the progression of the dementia, it may be worthwhile to consider adding one more piece of information to the tag, such as the relationship to the individual with dementia. For example, the tag could read:

John
(Your Son)

The primary caregiver, in making this assessment, needs to consider the individual with dementia's potential reaction to the tags. Some individuals may become angry, as if you are doing this to embarrass them. Perhaps you could prepare them for this change in the environment before it becomes necessary, by suggesting the benefit of this kind of cue. If you indicate that the name tags are helpful to you, then the individual with dementia will be less likely to see them as a label of his own failure.

Identify what you are doing with the name tags. Include a comment about how easy it is to say hello to a bank teller, a policeman, or anyone else who wears a name tag at their place of work. And remember to say that they are helpful to you when you meet people you may not know or recognize. Normalizing the use of name tags can go a long way toward helping the individual with dementia relax about seeing them on people in the home.

This use of name tags may not be necessary for spouses or children who visit frequently, but it may be very helpful for grandchildren who are rarely in the house visiting, or for old friends that come visit from afar. Here is where the small addition of identifying information on the name tag can be extraordinarily helpful. They provide help for the individual with dementia in identifying visitors who are extended family, for ministers that might visit, or for neighbors who might still want to come by for tea or to help in the garden.

Preparing the Visitors

Once again, from the point of view of preparing the environment, visitors are a new factor in the environment. We need to prepare those visitors because they become part of the environment the moment they arrive.

A simple welcoming sheet with the necessary information and guidelines is all that is needed. If you know in advance that a visitor will be coming, it is helpful to send them the welcoming sheet (by email perhaps). That way, they have a chance to read and absorb the information. It prepares the visitors for their entry into the environment without an on-the-spot need for repeated explanations by the primary caregiver about the changes in the house.

Preparing visitors with a welcoming sheet is another environmental preparation intended to eliminate some of the caregiver's stress. With that sheet, caregivers no longer have to deliver the same explanations to each person every time they visit, explanations that may be painful for the caregiver. Further, caregivers will no longer have to worry about remembering what to remind visitors about.

With this preparation, visitors will be more confident both about what to do and what not to do. Reducing their uncertainty means that their body language will telegraph more confidence to the person they are visiting. This opens wider the gates for positive interactions. It will further support the individual with dementia as well as the caregiver. It will also make it more likely that the visitors will feel comfortable and so wish to return.

We have included in the footnote below a link to our sample one-page welcoming guide you can use as a template for your own welcoming message. You can also simply use it as is.[1]

The Benefits in Institutional Settings

Just as this approach of cuing will prove beneficial in the home environment, it will also prove beneficial in an institutional setting. For example, having name tags for all residents allows them to recognize and to more smoothly interact with one another – at the dining table, in a small group having tea, or when engaging in an activity.

Having color-coded name tags for staff that differ from those for residents allows residents to more easily identify staff support. It enables residents to engage staff by name as well as making it possible for staff, even new hires, to speak to residents by name. The simple ability to address someone by name is a powerful bridge to establishing and maintaining everyday communications and putting everyone more at ease.

---

1 Our guide is available in several languages at www.montessorialzheimersproject.com.

Those without dementia are habituated to learning and remembering the names of people they interact with on an ongoing basis. They generally recognize the power of a cuing name tag when they are surrounded by people they don't know. We must remember that not being able to access the name of someone right in front of you is the experience of individuals with dementia every day, even with people they have known for years.

We have used the scenario of greetings to introduce the Montessori basic principles of Observation, humility, and cuing in the context of dementia care. There is a simplicity that we can engender in the dementia environment as it relates to communicating with others.

The purpose of beginning with greetings is to show that there are simple adjustments to the environment that can make those with dementia feel safer, that can make them feel that they are not being tested every moment. Similar adjustments are possible throughout the environment, all of which are targeted at changing the environment from one filled with obstacles to one that invites ease.

It is recovering that sense of ease rather than the sense of being surrounded by obstacles that makes individuals with dementia feel more at home and more part of their family and community. Fundamentally, it is a kind and achievable thing to do.

The Montessori Alzheimer's Project

Notes

Chapter 3 - Expanding Supportive Environments: Speech

Having examined the importance of Observation and of preparing the environment in the context of greetings, we now consider extending these principles into everyday communications beyond initial greetings.

This extension is important because the ability to safely engage in everyday interactions happens through communication. Communication makes our lives workable or unworkable. Everyday communications are fundamental to many of the critical interactions that give our lives order and meaning.

A key Montessori insight is that human beings have a fundamental need to do meaningful work. We are all looking for meaning in our lives, beginning in childhood and continuing throughout our lives. This does not end with a diagnosis of dementia. Order and meaning are relevant to everyone involved in dementia care, just as they are relevant to ordinary life.

We experience positive pride and joy when we are able to accomplish a meaningful task. We experience frustration and discontent when we are unable to do so. This is true for children in a classroom, for adults at work, for family members at home, and for individuals who have dementia. It is true for all human beings.

A basic Montessori principle is to purposefully maximize the effectiveness of the environment to support a child's developmental needs. In Montessori education, classrooms are set up with everything at child height, and everything is scaled to the size of the children. Montessori environments include a range of tasks designed so that children can accomplish meaningful work. This is the essence of Montessori learning. The key point is that the classroom's design and ongoing modifications are based on Observation. The starting point is the children's identified developmental needs. Modifications are based on continuing Observations of children as their developmental needs change.

In that same way, we can to maximize the effectiveness of the environment prepared for someone suffering from dementia. Again, Observation is the foundation to establish, and to be able to modify, the supportive environment on an ongoing, as-needed basis.

We all have roles in our immediate world, whether one is as a doctor, a cook, a cleaner, an entertainer, and so on. We have our image of being self-reliant in the different situations that make up our lives, whether it is at work, driving to the grocery store, or managing the checkbook. These are just some of the examples that are part of a person's life experience. For all of these tasks, we use the capacities we have developed to successfully complete them.

As we observe an individual with dementia, we see that the ability to continue functioning in those roles has begun to diminish. Our response to this, and the associated need for us to be able to better recognize these changes, highlights the importance of Observation. Let's continue our analysis by examining speech and non-verbal communication as indicated by one's demeanor.

Shifting the Focus from Words to Demeanor

We develop speech patterns over our lifetime. We learn accepted speech patterns, particularly within our immediate family and with close friends. We use these patterns again and again as routine ways through which we connect with, push away, or ignore people. With the onset and progression of dementia, there are changes, sometimes subtle ones, in speech patterns.

When we talk about changes in speech patterns, we are referring to patterns that go beyond the search for words that simply don't come to mind. Observing someone with dementia in a more arms-length and focused manner, we find that other changes in communication often occur. These changes can be less apparent to a more casual observer.

Passive Listening

For an individual with dementia who might have always participated fully in the give and take of conversations, there may be a shift towards more of a listening mode than was evident before. There might be a failure to follow the threads of a conversation, perhaps an ever-increasing drifting of attention that was never a problem before. Commonly, with Observation, it is clear that the individual with dementia is focusing ever more intently on body language and tone rather than content.

How do these shifts reveal themselves? It often begins with the individual using fewer words and more nods. There are simpler sentence structures. There are less frequent and shorter contributions to the conversation. These shorter contributions are usually responding to the other person's apparent request for affirmation about one point or another. There are more responses of "uh huh" or "mmmm" with an appropriate movement of the head.

When you notice this shift, observe further how the decision made by the individual with dementia is probably seen as an appropriate response to that cue in the conversation. You will observe that the individual is responding to the cues provided by the person speaking.

You can perform a simple experiment to confirm this by having a conversation with a friend. Try to say very little. Just look directly at them, nod, and make some of those "uh huh" or "mmmm" sounds with an appropriate movement of your head when your friend leaves a gap in the speech.

It is quite possible that your friend won't become aware of any problem, or of what you are doing at all. So far as they are concerned, they will assume you are just acknowledging the correctness of their statements. The nods, smiles, uh-huhs, and so forth are accepted as affirmation by the speaker as a response to the content rather than what they truly are – your response to a cue.

Instead of conversation, which is usually seen as volleys back and forth about the topic among the participants, there is no return volley when one person in the conversation has dementia. "Conversation" transitions to just one person speaking and one passively appearing to listen. That appearance of passive listening, and reacting in a non-confrontational way, is seen as agreement.

Increased Reliance on Body Language

This switch to passive listening also shows up in the body. The changes are subtle at the beginning. So it is important to focus and observe.

As we listen to someone else in conversation, our eyes really only stayed fixed upon each other briefly. (Perhaps a bit longer if we are talking about a particularly intense topic.) When the conversation is not intense, our eyes move to other places around the room, then back to the speaker. We return our gaze to the speaker to cue him that we are still paying attention. Depending on other body language, perhaps we cue that we wish to say something ourselves.

This is not so much the case for individuals with dementia. Because of the shift of focus toward body language, individuals with dementia in the early stages usually maintain their eye focus on the speaker. This helps them to more effectively read the speaker's body language as they become more reliant on that to cue their responses.

As dementia progresses, they cannot maintain even that focus. The healthy speaker often will try to bring the individual with dementia back into the conversation, trying to regain that missing eye contact and the affirming nods. The result is that the missing volleys in conversation become more noticeable, more frequently.

Engage with Simplicity

Let's step back for a moment and consider the guidance we can obtain from these Observations.

It is important to recognize and remember that individuals with dementia often experience a simple conversation as a test, as we discussed with regard to greetings. While conversation is usually not a test for us, it is important to refrain from denying the validity of the person with dementia's very different experience.

There are clearly things that we can do to support those with dementia as they attempt to deal with their experience of tests. The main point is, as always, to establish a sense of ease for the individual with dementia. Always remain aware that this sense of being tested can arise even in the simplest of conversational interactions.

The basic technique was presented in our previous discussion of greetings: simply give identifying information immediately, whether as a part of the greeting or of subsequent conversation.

Then, as the conversation unfolds, we can embark upon an expansion of this information, using the same approach. This involves clarifying the content by providing more information, while avoiding non-essential side notes.

In the discussion on greeting, we pointed out that giving the cues to the relationship was a direct support. You identify yourself and your relationship with the person who has dementia. Extending that initial bridge of understanding through further cues and protective adjustments in your speech patterns creates an increasingly richer and safer-feeling prepared environment for that person.

Beyond the greetings scenario, consider what you can do to provide additional cues to the individual with dementia. Those cues will make everyone's life easier. The essence of using language is to convey information. For individuals with dementia, we want to do that in as simple and as uncomplicated a form as possible with each sentence that we utter.

Observe people chatting in their everyday conversations. They generally do not speak in simple sentences. They do not communicate using a clear subject, verb, and object format. Instead, they speak in a somewhat circular way without always clearly identifying what they are discussing.

Without that clear identification, there is no obvious cue as to where they are heading in the conversation. They might use numerous modifying clauses and phrases, often in self-referential patterns. For communication like this to be successful, everyone's understanding of past speech patterns and conventions is required.

But, the recollection of those complex patterns and subtle conventions are often early casualties for a person with dementia. Therefore, caregivers and others sharing the space with an individual with dementia need to adjust their speech patterns. Start by looking directly at them when you speak. Then, speak just a bit more slowly than your customary pace.

This invites the individual with dementia to more easily identify that you are speaking to them. It enables them to follow the communication more easily. Just as importantly, it continually reminds you to maintain your changed speech patterns for their benefit.

While there is some effort associated with making those changes, the rewards for caregivers and visitors are enormous because the connection to the individual with dementia is supported. It is <u>you</u> bridging some of their difficulties.

With connection, warmth is more easily communicated, as is confidence in the relationship that you share.

So:

- Use simple sentences with very few modifiers.
- Eliminate irrelevant information.
- Avoid multiple clauses; make each one into a shorter sentence of its own.
- Organize sentences so that they flow logically in a direct sequence rather than circuitously.

The Montessori Alzheimer's Project

Let's see how following these recommendations might impact a real conversation.

This:

> *I saw Johnny yesterday, while I was driving my car down Main Street towards the old Miller building, which I heard they're going to knock down later in the year so that they can build a condominium tower. Why would they do that? Who needs more condos here?*
>
> *Anyway, I called him when I got home, and we talked for hours about how the two of us used to be so inseparable and how you used to drive us to the Friday dances every week because his father had abandoned the family, which meant that his mother had to stay home in the evenings to take care of Suzie and Jack. Jack was adopted, wasn't he?*
>
> *Johnny said to give you his love and that he'd come around to visit you soon, but not right away because he's due to go back on active duty on Saturday, and he'll probably be deployed to Europe or to Japan, neither of which would be his first choice – he wants to go to Central America this time, but there's not much chance of that apparently because he has a new C.O. – he'll get confirmation of where he's going tomorrow or maybe the day after.*

... Becomes this:

I saw Johnny yesterday.

He talked about how you used to drive us to the dance every week.

Johnny said to give you his love.

He's being deployed overseas next week.

He said he'd come and visit you when he gets back.

Consider the effort needed to read the first version of the communication. You did it, but it took a fair amount of energy and attention. You had to identify which of the many bits of information was relevant to the point being made. Then, consider the ease of reading the second version.

The second had no diversions off the topic. There were no complicated sentences strung together, thought after thought. There were no sentences unrelated to the intended message.

Keep your words simple, focused and direct. It is of critical importance that the interaction be one more of ease than of obstacle. The message will more likely get through and an actual conversation is more likely to occur.

The Importance of Body Language

We often use and read subtle body language to see where people are heading in conversation,. And just as often, our eyes wander around the room. We come back to focus on another person as we make a particular point. We do this to cue them of its importance as well as to assure ourselves that they are paying attention.

The understanding of subtle body language is another casualty in the early progression of dementia. As our eyes wander, the individual with dementia may follow the direction of our gaze. Why would that be? It is because our gaze is cuing that behavior. To the individual with dementia, the cue infers that there is something important to be seen wherever we may be looking. This disengages them from the conversation. It also prevents them from picking up other cues from the speaker. Because they are looking in a different direction, they are no longer looking at the speaker for more cues.

It is no surprise that someone with dementia will feel tested in those situations. They will, perhaps, withdraw from involvement in the conversation. They may simply wait for a cue to tell them to nod one way or the other.

We can support the individual with dementia in conversation by modifying our own customary conduct.

When we look directly at the individual we're speaking to, it is a cue that you are speaking directly to them. People who have dementia need this cue, so maintain eye contact during the conversation. If you keep the sentence structure short, direct and simple, gentle eye contact is all that is needed. It is friendly rather than challenging.

Don't let your gaze wander much, even if this is your normal tendency. At the same time, don't fixedly stare at them because that is a different kind of cue. In a relaxed way, simply re-engage with their eyes more often than you would have done in the past.

As was said before, looking away as you talk can be interpreted by the person with dementia as a cue that they should be looking in that same direction. It might also be a cue that their participation in the conversation is over. If that is what they take from your looking away, you can try to bring them back into the conversation gently, by using their name, for example. Otherwise, there is a good chance they will experience the intended conversation as another failed test.

So:

- Maintain gentle eye contact throughout the conversation.
- Gently hold the other person's hand(s) or touch their shoulder while you're speaking.
- Use the person's name periodically, but naturally, as you talk.

These are all clear, positive cues that invite and maintain connection. They help to ground the individual with dementia in the warmth of the communication.

The Montessori Alzheimer's Project

Notes

Chapter 4 - Preparing the Environment: The Kitchen

There are key Montessori principles that can be used to guide caregivers in setting up any environment to guide individuals with dementia. We are looking to provide guidance for their safety as well as to facilitate their mastery of tasks to the extent their then-current capabilities. Starting with Observation, we look to apply the 3 S's: Standardize, Simplify and provide Signage.

So, preparing a kitchen environment to protect someone with dementia begins, once again, with Observation. Because there are dangers in a kitchen, we need to use Observation to help us understand how an individual with dementia might engage with that environment. In this way, we gain insight into preparing it for their safety and then, for their ease. The kitchen is a focal point in most households as preparing food and eating it is an activity that most families join in.

So, observe the kitchen and the related dining environment. Our objective is to evaluate the environment and identify the steps in each of the tasks that take place in that environment. The Montessori insight here is to establish an environment that provides guidance throughout the task. This enables us to provide cues so that these common tasks are safer and more accessible to the individual with dementia.

Why should we be particularly interested in everyday tasks? It is because these are the tasks that give our lives order and meaning. Being able to engage with them makes our lives workable, putting us at ease. Being unable to engage with them makes our lives much less workable, creating the sense of obstacles rather than ease.

The kitchen clearly presents elements of danger for the individual with dementia. This is true for all of us of course. But, the dangers increase as an individual with dementia's powers of discrimination, reasoning, and understanding deteriorate.

Eliminate Dangers

The first priority is to protect the individual from the dangers associated with stoves and stovetop burners. People without dementia sometimes forget that they have left the stovetop on, and that something is cooking. This leads to burned pots and pans.

Usually, we are warned of danger by the smell of smoke before it becomes something quite serious involving burns or fires. This is because people without dementia understand environmental cues, such as the smell of burning foods and pots. Cues such as the smell of gas or burning food click into the normal response of ensuring that the gas is turned off. Seeing a bright red electric element is a cue that it is terribly hot and needs to be turned off.

Individuals with dementia will not necessarily understand or react to those cues that we take for granted. Therefore, it is important to modify the environment to eliminate the risks. If we are unable to eliminate those risks, we need to provide additional, more accessible cues appropriate to the individual with dementia.

Preparing a kitchen environment by eliminating risks takes precedence over preparing the environment through cuing. Elimination of risk is more protective of everyone, not just the individual with dementia but caregivers and other family members. This is critical because an unsafe kitchen puts everyone in the house, as well as those outside the house, at risk.

If you have an electric stove, install a master switch so that the individual with dementia cannot turn on the stove simply by touching the usual buttons and knobs. An electrician can add a somewhat out of the way on/off switch that caregivers can use to turn the controls on or off, away from the stove itself.

Anyone who wishes to cook must first turn on that master switch. They can cook and then turn the master switch off when they are finished. This enhances safety, as the individual with dementia is unlikely to learn or to retain the information that cooking now requires the use of this new switch to make the stove work.

With this provision in place, the individual with dementia cannot simply turn on the stove elements or the oven and then forget to turn them off. The heating elements just won't work because the electrical circuit is now controlled first by the master switch.

If you have a gas stove, you may decide to replace it with an electric one modified as suggested above. If you want to continue using a gas stove, or don't have an option about it, make sure that it is one that will not release the gas unless the ignition is on or the flame is lit. This is a more common safety feature on newer gas stoves. For older ones, perhaps having a gas cut-off valve installed would be best. This type of cut-off works along the same lines as the electrical cut-off switch described above. However, if the stove operates on a pilot light, it would require lighting the stove at each use.

Another new technology alternative is an induction stovetop. This only works when an iron pan is in place. It turns off automatically when the pan is removed, and the stovetop quickly cools. Without a pan on it, the element cannot heat up nor can it remain on. No iron pan, no heat.

To boil water to make coffee or tea, use an electric kettle that automatically turns itself off after boiling the water. This is safer than heating water in a pot on the stove.

Each of these suggestions is focused on changing the environment to support safety and the individual with dementia. You are adjusting the environment to meet his needs rather than demanding that he adjust to the environment.

Look for any other issues in the kitchen that may hold danger for an individual with dementia. Adjust the environment to eliminate the potential dangers you observe. That is the first task.

The Montessori Alzheimer's Project

Cuing the Kitchen

Once you have reviewed and prepared the kitchen environment for safety, it is time to prepare the environment with cues. The cues should be designed to support the individual with dementia so as to enable participation in ongoing meaningful household work. This supports an individual with dementia's self-esteem and feelings of connection to everyday life.

When we look at our own kitchen, everything is familiar. We know where the pots are kept, and what is in the refrigerator. We remember what is behind the closed cabinet doors. But if we walk into someone else's kitchen, we may not be so confident.

If we are at someone else's house, we might open one cabinet door after another looking for a water glass, for example. We would keep opening doors until we located where this other family keeps their glassware. We will likely prioritize which cabinets to check first. We look into our memory for typical placements of glasses/cups in kitchen cabinets we've encountered in the past.

We might guess correctly the very first time. We wouldn't feel uncomfortable if we had to open 2 or 3 more cabinets while looking, because it is a new environment for us. After a few visits to that other kitchen, we would likely remember the cabinet in which water glasses are kept.

Now, imagine the stress of having to do that every time you entered your own kitchen. That kitchen is supposed to be so familiar to you. After all, you have entered this kitchen every day for years. Yet, for the individual with dementia, cabinet after cabinet needs to be opened, every time.

Where once one could easily identify, find, and use various kitchen supplies, an individual with dementia begins to experience increasing difficulty. Often, in the process of opening the cabinets, they may forget what they are looking for. This results in even more frustration, and it happens every day, potentially every time that individual goes into the kitchen looking for something.

Avoiding Frustration

The question is clear: How might we cue the kitchen environment so the individual with dementia can function successfully in his own home with minimum stress? We need to take into account that as dementia progresses, the ability to self-organize perceptions into meaningful information becomes weaker and weaker. So, we want to create cues that will build upon each other now and, as needed, in the future.

There are key Montessori approaches for preparing and modifying the environment in order to accommodate these difficulties: *Standardize, Simplify*. These ideas enable us to modify the environment so as to limit the opportunities for frustration. They enable the individual with dementia to be guided within a more easily managed perceptual field, one which is easier for him to engage. *Standardization* and *simplification* make *signage* cues (see below) more effective.

The Montessori Alzheimer's Project

Once we have standardized and simplified the environment, the next stage is to create *Signage*. The signage itself should be standardized and simplified as well. This third principle guides our completion of the basic process of kitchen modification.

Each modification must be grounded in practical implementation of these ideas to create a supportive environment. While everyone's home is a bit different, these principles are widely applicable.

How to Standardize

Take a look in the kitchen cabinets. Are there a fair number of mugs and cups? Do they have many shapes, colors and sizes? Some with saucers and some without? Standardize them, so there is just one type in the cabinet. Then place them on the same shelf each time.

No other items should be mixed with them. In other words, all the mugs are together. If you have glasses on that same shelf, again, standardize them and group them on a separate shelf if possible. If it is not possible, group them on the other side of the shelf so that mugs and glasses are isolated, unmixed with each other.

Do you have multiple sizes and shapes of plates and bowls? Again, standardize. The differences may have been a delight in the past, but circumstances are changing. Now, and into the future as your loved one's condition becomes more challenging, the differences will begin to present obstacles to him. If you cannot pare down to one size, eliminate the sizes that are rarely used. Again, physically isolate the different shapes and sizes from each other.

You will likely have time to gradually implement these kinds of changes. As always, Observation will guide you to what is needed based on assessing the then-current abilities of your loved one. If he has just been diagnosed, he can help you with these preparations.

Remember to introduce this kind of task by referring to how it will be helping you. Make the focus on you rather than highlighting the growing needs of the individual with dementia. This is a simple kind of redirection, another key Montessori principle that will be addressed in more detail later. In short, you are redirecting the individual with dementia's attention to something more likely to put him at ease rather than forcing him to confront his declining abilities.

Whittle away at each potential confusion. Add refinements to the environment along the above lines until you have standardized everything wherever there is a non-essential choice to make.

Simplify

Eliminate the excess in the kitchen. Simplicity is less taxing. If you are able to simplify the contents of your kitchen like this, the individual with dementia is less likely to be overwhelmed by the number of choices as well as by the size or the intensity of the perceptual display.

The Montessori Alzheimer's Project

You probably have more things in your kitchen than you need for your daily life. Most people do. Look in your kitchen cabinets and drawers with the keen eye of Observation.

You can look, for example, to assess:

- How many knives, forks, and spoons are in the kitchen drawer?
- How many plates, cups, bowls?
- How many kitchen towels?
- How many placemats?
- How many coffee mugs?
- How many teacups?
- How many water glasses?

Every excess item can become a source of confusion for your loved one, so simplify. Pack away extras that are rarely needed. Just keep enough of each item for the number of people who live and generally visit in your home. It may be just two or three of each: One for the caregiver, one for the person who is being cared for and one or maybe two for visitors. Keep the items that are used for visitors at the very back of the shelf with just the ones used every day at the front. Store additional pieces of each item out of sight, ready to be brought out when there are more guests.

Fewer things means that the environment is less likely to be overwhelming for the person with dementia. It means fewer opportunities for confusion, uncertainty, and mistakes. These changes minimize stress by eliminating unimportant options that divert attention. Less stress means more ease, which makes life better for everyone.

Signage: Display Cues

Having first gone through the standardization and then simplification of items in the kitchen, simple signage cues become more meaningful and more potent as a support. Place a picture of the each particular item that is inside a cabinet on the outside of the cabinet door.

The picture should be at the height of the shelf on which the item is kept. This is a cue that is a bridge between the object being looked for and where the object actually is. In this way, the cabinet door becomes a support in the environment rather than an obstacle hiding the item from the individual.

The idea is to create a guided path that leads to a successful completion of the particular task at hand – such as looking for a cup. While no solution will be completely failure-proof by first standardizing, then simplifying, and finally using clear signage, the environment limits potential choices. Limiting the choices limits the potential for failure. Limiting the potential for failure leads to more positive outcomes throughout the day.

Clear printed signs for the cabinet doors can be utilized at an early stage. Printed signs with pictures might be needed to replace them later. Just signs with pictures may be useful at an even later stage.

The Montessori Alzheimer's Project

Looking for a teacup? Signage provides the necessary cues. The cabinet door is opened, and the answer to the task is right there. If there are only two teacups on a shelf, it makes setting the table for tea free of most potential obstacles. A mix of text and image mutually reinforces the message once text alone is no longer sufficient.

As the dementia progresses, you may decide to remove the cupboard doors altogether. This allows for the items in the cabinet to be clearly observed the minute anyone enters the room. This is when the power of standardization and simplification alone is demonstrated, as it eliminates as many opportunities for confusion as possible.

Some might look at this use of signage as demeaning. As you deal with this perception, consider that many adults use this approach when learning a new language. Before going on a trip to a foreign country, adult travelers often post signs in their own home in that foreign language. They do this to reinforce their understanding and memory. It promotes repetition, an important factor in the learning process.

The signage we recommend provides that reinforcement and repetition for individuals with dementia. It is a support to enable them to retain as much of their capacity to self-manage in the environment as possible.

In summary, organize everything commonly used in the kitchen area (as well as in the rest of your house over time) in an orderly, predictable way. To the extent possible, separate everything physically. Prepare cued places for each different item or group of items. This makes it easier for your loved one to find what he needs. Giving him the support he needs allows him to help himself as well as to help you by minimizing difficulties caused by the dementia.

At first, your kitchen cabinets and drawers will look a little sparse to you. They will also look that way to a visitor. Drawers and cupboards may seem to be empty enough to create an echo. But, you'll have taken positive steps toward creating an environment geared to be functional for the individual with dementia.

Why is this so important? Because the individual with dementia has a declining ability to manage sensory input. You are adjusting the amount and quality of that input. You are supporting individuals with dementia so that they will be less likely to be overwhelmed by the available choices. In short, it eliminates much of the testing experiences of life with dementia.

The MAP approach is about making independent life possible and joyful for you together with the one you love. When you *standardize* and *simplify*, when you cue the environment with *signage*, life together becomes less stressful. Ultimately, you preserve connection, more of what is possible and joyful for you both.

The Montessori Alzheimer's Project

Notes

The Montessori Alzheimer's Project

Chapter 5 - The Prepared Environment for Meals

You have carefully studied the kitchen environment, and the outcomes of your Observations have made it possible for you to make the cooking area in the kitchen safe. Then, you standardized the cabinets and drawers, simplifying that aspect of the kitchen environment. Finally, you made it more user-friendly for individuals with dementia by adding simple signage.

Now, we need to assess how this prepared environment can be further used to address the fundamental need to do meaningful work. That need still applies to individuals with dementia, just as it does to everyone. In this chapter, we now discuss the opportunities for meaningful work connected with both cooking and serving meals, which both offer opportunities for engagement to the individual with dementia.

Consider what is needed to prepare the environment so as to enable someone with dementia to accomplish meal-related tasks. To do that work safely, with a sense of ease and as a meaningful contribution to the daily household routine without experiencing it as a test, is a hugely positive foundation for life at home for an individual with dementia.

Muscle Memory

As we are now discussing the application of Montessori principles to tasks that involve the use of muscles, it is important to point out that we all retain the memory of physical sequences that we have repeated throughout our lives. Some of these tasks involve physical movements that we have indeed done many times in the past. These sequences can be triggered, accessed, and used in the context of caring for someone with dementia.

Briefly speaking, muscle memory is the memory of a physical pattern, a sequence of muscles that engage in a particular order each time we repeat a task. Muscle memory is activated when we engage our muscles in a sequence or pattern that is imprinted into our muscles and nervous system by that repetition. The sequence is remembered in a way that is not undermined in the same fashion or at the same time as memory related to facts or ideas. It is the equivalent of a muscular autopilot.

Being able to ride a bicycle for the first time in several years is an example of triggering muscle memory. If you ever learned to ride a bicycle, you don't get on a bike and have to think out what to do, how to balance, and when to pedal. None of this is based on conceptual understanding. Eating with a fork or spoon is another task that is ingrained into muscle memory. Triggering muscle memory means that you trigger old sequences preserved within your body that are independent of explicit conceptual memory.

When we look at tasks to successfully engage the individual with dementia, tying the guidance into muscle memory can be an extraordinary support. Muscular repetition supports the completion of the task, whether it is toileting, gardening, sewing, or eating. Maintaining and re-engaging muscle memory is a powerful tool for support.[2]

The Montessori Alzheimer's Project

This approach demonstrates how, first with Observation and then with modification of your home, coupled with the triggering of simple muscle memory, you can extend the duration of a safe, stable, and joyful life at home for the individual with dementia. As we analyze and adjust environments, finding triggers for muscle memory can help bring the satisfaction of successful daily life to both the individual and the caregiver.

Self-Correcting Environments

Looking to Montessori methods once again to provide guidance, we see that in Montessori-prepared environments for children, classroom tasks utilize carefully organized materials. Materials are set up to be used in sequential ways that are self-correcting.

The tasks provide feedback that indicates whether actions taken are headed in the direction of success or in a direction that requires a change in approach. The materials and the environment are, in effect, self-correcting.

As a result, the task itself is structured so as to inherently guide to the optimum result.

Setting the Table

Let's consider a few common meal-related tasks. Start with the task of setting the table for a meal. This happens a few

---

2 For a wonderful example using the power of muscle memory in dementia care, see https://www.youtube.com/watch?v=WkJc2Rk6IgA

times each day. Consider how the individual with dementia can accomplish this task.

Your simplified kitchen cabinets make it much easier for the individual with dementia to get out plates and cutlery in the correct number from their more easily identified places in the cabinets. Use placemats on which plates, cutlery, glasses, and napkins are outlined. These provide a placement guide so that the table can be set with little assistance from you. [3]

Setting the table is a meaningful everyday task which supports self-esteem and connection. It is a contribution to the home activity of sharing a meal. And, it is something that happens repeatedly. It is a habit that can be reclaimed if necessary, and reinforced by meaningful repetition a few times each day.

Preparing a Meal

As for preparing the meal, start with remembering that teamwork is one of the joyful aspects of cooking. Keep the cooking simple. However, we know that even simple cooking requires a several items and usually involves a number of sequenced tasks.

Here is a presentation of a self-correcting cooking activity: preparing toast and scrambled eggs for breakfast.

---

[3] https://www.parents.com/fun/printables/other/table-setting-place-mats/

The Montessori Alzheimer's Project

Based on Observation, we begin by breaking down the sequence of actions that are necessary to successfully make toast.

Most toasters have a timer that can be preset for light, medium, or dark toast. Once the caregiver has set that control, there is no opportunity for burning the toast.

Most toasters also have slots for either 2 or 4 pieces of toast. This limited number of toasting slots keeps the task both simple and self-correcting for the individual with dementia. If the individual with dementia has difficulty locating the bread and/or removing slices, the caregiver sets out the correct number of slices beside the toaster.

The individual with dementia can only fill each slot in the toaster once, no more than that, because only one piece of bread fits into each slot. This is the essence of self-correction. Each piece of bread, and only one piece, fits into a slot.

Toasters have what Montessori would call a "visual control of error." The top section of each slice can be observed in each slot, so empty slots are obvious. Also, once a slot is filled, there is no room for another slice of bread (a Montessori "physical control of error"), so one is led to the next empty slot where muscle memory may be triggered to fill it. Limiting the number of slices of bread will define the end of the sequence of filling the toaster.

Once the toaster slots are filled, again muscle memory may be triggered to push the lever down, and the toaster is started. If the next step of starting the toaster isn't triggered, guiding the "downward push" that starts the toast on its way may be all that is necessary to reclaim or reinforce the muscle memory. The toaster then safely completes the toasting task.

The caregiver may need to intervene when the newly toasted bread is ready to be taken out from the toaster. This will depend upon the capabilities of the individual for whom they are caring. There will likely be no need at first, but later on assistance may be needed so that the possibility of burns is avoided.

If butter on the toast is desired, organizing and sequencing can make an enormous difference here also. Consider how much easier it is to spread butter on toast, hot or cooled, when the butter is already softened. If the butter is very cold, it will not spread easily for anyone, whether or not they have dementia.

Once again, muscle memory should be invited, encouraged, and exercised in the spreading of the softened butter. Exercising those fine motor skills will have benefits for other tasks involving those same muscles in a slightly different remembered sequence.

With these preparations, you simplify the task. As the caregiver, you simplify the tasks of buttering toast by taking the butter out of the refrigerator first. This preparation results in the butter warming and softening a bit before it is needed. This eliminates frustration in the task of spreading the butter. Eliminating potential frustration is always a positive.

The Montessori Alzheimer's Project

So:

- Place the butter knife next to the butter dish.
- Set out one plate for each person.
- Place the plates next to the toaster so it is clear where the toast is placed when it pops up.
- If you limit the bread to one slice per person, then again the task is simplified.
- Place the butter and butter knife together after the toast is put on the plates, which invites the physical sequence of actions that come next.

In the same way, break down the sequence of making scrambled eggs. Organize the task first:

- Set out the number of eggs to scramble.
- Set out the mixing bowl and the whisk or fork for stirring the eggs.
  (By taking these first two steps, you have already limited potential problems.)
- The individual with dementia can set the required number of dinner plates out close to the stovetop because that part of the environment has already been modified to support that action.
- The individual with dementia can crack all the eggs into the mixing bowl.
- The eggs are whisked or stirred.
- The caregiver can get the pan, the butter, and the spatula while the whisking is done.
- The caregiver heats up the pan and melts the butter in it.

- The individual with dementia can pour the whisked eggs into the heated pan.
- The caregiver turns the mixture as the eggs cook.
- When the eggs are cooked, the caregiver places them onto the waiting plates, which limits the individual with dementia's contact with a hot pan.
- The individual with dementia takes the filled plates up and places them on the table.
- You have a great meal, prepared and eaten together.

The fact is that scrambled eggs prepared in this way always seem to taste better because they are made with love – the most important ingredient – by two people working in concert together.

Invite the individual with dementia to do as many or as few of the sequenced tasks as appropriate to their then-capacity. So long as there is participation, there will likely be both satisfaction and an increase in self-esteem.

These examples highlight the value of organizing and sequencing meaningful tasks. This approach allows the individual with dementia to participate in the ongoing tasks of daily life. For most people, preparing meals is part of their everyday routines, a framework for the day. These are examples of how to preserve these routines in the lives of our loved ones who have dementia.

One Task at a Time

Of course, cooking can be far more complex than what is required for scrambled eggs. But by applying these principles, one can usually identify the aspects of any kitchen task that can be broken down. Some of these can then be organized as single tasks to be done in sequence. This facilitates the successful participation of the individual with dementia. Coupled with setting the dining table, mealtimes can be a constant, consistent, and positive contribution by your loved one to the household routine.

Before becoming a caregiver, there was no reason to first count slices of bread or eggs and then to set them in the work area. There was no need to establish an organized, self-corrective scaffold for successful completion of meaningful tasks by our loved one. Now, with a little bit of planning and organizing, we create vehicles for maintaining connection, affection, and joy in daily life. Again we see that by changing some of our own habits, we can support the individual with dementia in kitchen and dining tasks.

In the kitchen, as elsewhere, structure each activity according to the principle of one task at a time. Remember that by slowing down and observing, we can break down each identifiable task into its step-by-step components. Then, we organize and lay out each sub-task in order. Ensuring that things happen sequentially means that we do not mix the tasks or any sub-tasks.

The idea is to limit the individual with dementia to one task or subtask at a time. In other words, to what is manageable at his then-current developmental state.

With the cues of ordered components and sequencing, we can support the abilities of the individual with dementia. We create meaningful tasks that are self-correcting whenever possible. Through Standardizing, Simplifying, Signage, and activation of Muscle Memory, the individual with dementia is guided toward success with as few obstacles as possible.

It is extraordinary to learn from experience that each time we establish meaning in our loved one's life, in the life of any individual with dementia, we engender meaning in our own lives. This is a fundamental spiritual component of caregiving. It is a path to living each and every day in the most positive uplifted way possible.

The Montessori Alzheimer's Project

Notes

The Montessori Alzheimer's Project

Chapter 6 - Applied Journaling

As caregivers, we empower our work based on the key Montessori principle of Observation. We do this by keeping a detailed journal. A journal enables us to record the many events that occur day-to-day which might otherwise be forgotten. We record what happens in our loved one's daily schedule to identify patterns in that schedule, to uncover patterns of behavior. In this way, the journal provides guidance to the practical application of Observation.

Having a journal allows you to monitor the consistency of daily life events. It enables you to identify changes that may be having an unsuspected impact upon the individual with dementia as well as you, the caregiver. These changes may be making life easier, they may be making it more difficult. Tracking the changes enables you to make those assessments.

With those assessments, we track the impact of any adjustments we then make to the environment. We can assess whether we need more Standardization or maybe more Simplification. We can determine whether improved Signage is needed or has helped.

<u>Journal Your Observations</u>

As caregivers, we begin by keeping a journal of daily events in the life of the individual with dementia. Here, "daily events" means what the person with dementia actually does throughout the day. It is not what has been planned out for them, it is what they actually do.

Especially in the beginning, journaling is not about scheduling events. It is about observing the event of the day and keeping a record of how the individual behaves throughout it. This is the source material we need to provide benefit.

Here are a few suggested points for Observation:

- When/where/how positive behavior occurs.
- When/where/how negative behavior occurs.
- The apparent objective of the behavior.
- Is the objective of the action/behavior clear.
- Is the objective of the behavior attained?
- Who is present, and who is absent, when the behavior occurs?
- What objects are being used in the activity?
- Are the objects being used correctly and, if not, how are they being used?
- What is the flow with others in joint activities?
- What is happening when the person with dementia engages with the environment?
- What is happening when the person with dementia disengages with the environment?

Based on those Observations, consider how the environment supports or impedes the needs being expressed. Recording the time of each activity and behavior is important. Why? Because behaviors can change according to the time of day.

Sometimes a behavior occurs at a particular time each day. This directs you to look at what might be triggering it, whether it is positive or negative behavior. The only way to make these connections is to scrupulously record the time and the specifics of the behavior.

When it is difficult to understand the purpose of a particular behavior (meaning the need the behavior is trying to address) think more broadly about the context. Look further for environmental triggers that might be present. Also look into the life experience of the individual to see if there is a connection that is hidden there.

Perhaps they always read the newspaper with breakfast. Perhaps they were avid gardeners, or always walked their dog after lunch. Maybe they liked to listen to music with afternoon tea.

If you can connect current conduct with something in the environment now, you may be able to adjust the environment to meet that need. If you can connect current conduct to their pre-dementia life, you may be able to successfully fulfill that need being expressed now knowing that its source is indicated by their past. For example, if they always folded laundry, include that as part of the daily or weekly activity. Folding it together as a joint project may be what is needed to give them a comfortable reference point. Considerations like this are all part of creating an environmental framework of support.

Start with the very first morning events. Observe how the morning unfolds. As your journal takes shape logging events both day and night, it becomes an ever more effective tool to identify issues and trends.

Wake-up usually occurs about the same time each day. Should the wake-up time change suddenly, a journal may allow you to consider what might be related to that change. You can see if something unusual happened the evening before.

Perhaps dinner was eaten late last night, or perhaps it was a particularly spicy meal. It could be that everyone stayed up too late the evening before. Maybe there was too much activity the evening before, too many people to deal with, and that resulted in agitation. Maybe agitation or sleeplessness is a side effect to a new medication – a side effect of which you were unaware.

On an ongoing basis, we review and reflect upon what we have recorded. With the information we have gathered, we modify the environment and our own behaviors to benefit the individual with dementia.

Journaling Related to Toileting

Upon awakening in the morning, the first thing one usually does is use the toilet. If that changes, a carefully maintained journal may enable you to identify what might be responsible for the change.

Beyond the wake-up morning routine toileting, a journal allows you to see patterns such as how many times – and when – toileting is necessary throughout the day. Again, changes in patterns can be important for identifying issues. The changes may indicate the need for modifying the environmental support. They may also suggest possible fundamental health changes to check for.

For example, if an individual with dementia becomes constipated, early intervention is quite important. It is unlikely that you will happen to remember when their last bowel movement occurred. Without that information, and the information about bowel movements over the past several days, you may not have the information needed to identify a potential problem. Your journal allows you to do that.

You can use your journal to support the individual with dementia through diet. It may be that the individual has not been eating any fiber. It may be that they need to be invited to consume more liquids. It may be that it really is an early warning to schedule a medical check-up.

You may not remember how much you yourself drink each day. It is even less likely that a person with dementia will remember how much they drank. But how do you know if they are drinking enough liquids? A journal is that critical resource tracking resource for caregiving here.

You may also find that by tracking the timing and quantity of liquids, you will be able to predict the timing of urination. The same goes for understanding the timing between eating meals and bowel movements. This information, once it is gathered, can be checked periodically (rather than every day) for ongoing accuracy.

This kind of journaled information can be extremely helpful in determining the best times for travel outside the home. Your journal records may tell you that the person with dementia usually has to urinate an hour after drinking a glass of water, or regularly has a bowel movement in the middle of the afternoon. Using that information, you can plan your trips outside the home to minimize potential toileting issues when outside the home.

Journaling may well give you important alerts to guide you in structuring the day. For example, if the person with dementia naps regularly in the mid-afternoon, this information guides you to avoid medical appointments, visitors, or outings during that time.

A key objective of the MAP program is to enable the person with dementia to remain at home for longer. Here, the proviso is that the home must be modified for safety and support. There will be a need for trips outside the home to doctors, the grocery store, or to your religious community. Use journaling to guide your scheduling of travel outside the home.

Journaling Liquids and Caffeine Intake

Keep track of liquid intake, and especially of how much caffeine is taken in during the day, whether from coffee, tea, chocolate, or soda pop. This can be very helpful in identifying the need for caffeine and perhaps for setting limits.

Why are limits important? A person with dementia doesn't immediately forget that they like coffee, chocolate, or soda pop the moment they are diagnosed. Lowering their average intake of caffeine, identified through your journaling, can be a gentle way to reduce caffeine in the diet.
This can be extremely helpful, as a major concern for caregivers is the tendency for individuals with dementia to get up and wander at night. Caffeine can exacerbate this behavior. Simply opting for decaffeinated coffee and tea, terminating caffeine intake earlier each evening may lessen night wandering, which would result in better sleep for everyone. It is also possible to begin transitioning evening coffee and tea to hot water with lemon or an herbal tea. This provides a physical cue of warm liquid in the belly that may ease the transition away from warm caffeinated drinks.

Coffee and tea, particularly green tea, are diuretics. Drinking these beverages may need to be balanced with glasses of water. Further, people with dementia will be unable to judge when they need to drink more water. As a result, dehydration can impact them both in body and mind. By tracking water intake and scheduling drinking water breaks, caregivers can protect the individual with dementia from the physical, emotional, and behavioral effects of dehydration.

Journaling and Sundowning

Many people with dementia experience "sundowning." Sundowning refers to the onset of confusion and agitation that happens in the late afternoon and early evening. It is a period of transition when daylight shifts to dusk, then to darkness as the sun sets. This transition time can provoke difficulties for a person with dementia.

Identifying sundowning is facilitated by journaling. Keep track of how often it happens, when it usually begins, and when it usually ends. This is all critical information to enable you to prepare the environment of support properly. This data allows the caregiver to adjust both the environment and the schedule to ease those difficulties.

When a caregiver identifies that sundowning will likely occur at a particular time each day, travel outside the home at that time can be avoided. Inside the home, the caregiver might schedule an activity that redirects the individual with dementia away from the triggers that invite this behavior. Knowing when sundowning generally begins allows the caregiver to adjust the environment before it impacts the individual with dementia.

Prior to the beginning of sundowning, the caregiver might turn on more inside lights while closing the curtains and blinds. Doing this before extra light is actually needed inside the home can make the outside lighting changes less impactful. Further, this may be a good time for the caregiver and the individual with dementia sit down together and listen to a favorite music playlist. This is a sedate activity that may invite warmth, rather than agitation.

Establishing a positive and proactive routine, beginning prior to the outdoor lighting shift that carries over past twilight, helps direct the individual with dementia toward positive behavior triggers. Whether it is listening to music together, playing cards or sketching together, directing attention to positive warm interactions before the sundowning behavior can arise tends to help avoid or at least limit its impact.

<u>Journaling and Media</u>

Many people have routines of watching television together. In fact, some people watch the same show every night. Note in your journal any reactions that are different than before. For example, perhaps there was no issue in the past when commercials play. There may now be an issue.

Sometimes, individuals with dementia are disturbed by the rapid visual shifts in commercials. Sometimes, they have difficult reconnecting with the story after a commercial interruption. Watching a favorite old movie or television show on Netflix or on DVD are ways to avoid the jangling commercial interruptions that undermine the ability of the individual with dementia to engage with the story.

Why is this the case? It is because there is a great difference in input coming at you during commercials – rapid cuts and random images coupled with increased volume – rather than a clear stable story that is constant from beginning to end.

Sometimes, even within television shows, there are heightened images and sounds screaming for your attention, for you to *"tune in tomorrow."* These kinds of sounds and images are absolutely not helpful to individuals with dementia.

Music can be used very effectively to trigger old, warm memories. Listen to CDs or use streaming services rather than the radio, again to avoid the jangling of commercials.

Creating a personal music playlist can help in so many ways. Listening to music from the early parts of one's life often triggers warm memories. Classical music also has the quality of engaging the ear with emotions a bit differently. It is positive even for individuals unaccustomed to classical music. Any music can also encourage movement, humming along, and experience of the simple pleasure of listening to beautiful sounds.

The information in your journal, over time, will help guide you as to when changes might be made, and what changes should be tried next.

Journaling and Exercise

Keep track of how much walking happens each day. Tracking the timing of naps and evening sleep can also be helpful. Too much exercise can be exhaustingly stressful. Not enough exercise may trap energy that needs to be expended to allow the individual with dementia to sleep.

Scheduling a walk or another activity that uses large muscle groups should take into account the customary timing of toileting needs and of sundowning. Taking that information into account makes walking more pleasant and far less stressful. This is another way that journaling can help you establish a safe routine.

We are suggesting that you consider modifying your own routines. If you do have a long routine of a late afternoon walk, consider whether it is worth shifting that walk to the early afternoon instead. While you may miss the gentle onset of twilight you enjoyed during your walks, consider the trade-off you would be making. If shifting the timing an hour or so avoids sundowning, there will be benefit for both the individual with dementia and for you as well.

The value of getting exercise and fresh air is well known. The value of avoiding the known difficulty of sundowning will become ever more clear as your experience its impact from the caregiving perspective. Scheduling may allow you to accommodate both exercise and protection from sundowning.

We have created a sample journal format that you can use as a simple checklist while you build your own journal.[4] You may of course prefer to use your own format. The point is that whatever format you use, your journal will help support both the caregiver and the person with dementia.

---

[4] The checklist is available for download at www.montessorialzheimersproject.com

Journaling for Use by Respite Caregivers

It is important to make sure that you have the time as a caregiver to be "off-duty." Every primary caregiver needs a break for their own well-being. A respite caregiver is the substitute for that primary caregiver, someone who can come in a be a temporary caregiver for a few hours or even a few days if needed.

Your journal will enable a respite caregiver to far more easily slip into the caregiver mode smoothly and safely. It will enhance the respite caregiver's understanding and awareness of that individual with dementia. The respite caregiver will be guided in providing care by the journal-identified needs of the individual with dementia.

The journal and/or the schedule that you create based on your journal, gives the respite caregiver an effective tool. It is a tool that also engenders confidence in their ability to provide appropriate care while the primary caregiver gets their needed break. It can support the person with dementia's feelings of safety even when the primary caregiver is away.

Make sure respite caregivers take the time before arriving to review the guidance for all visitors. Have a name tag for them already prepared. Use your journal to highlight the routine for that day or that period of the day.

A journal enables the respite caregiver to see and to fit into the routine of the person with dementia. This is much better than having the caregiver guess the needs and routine of the person with dementia. It is the journal that allows you to be away knowing that basic and key caregiving information is in place.

Look at the journal together with the respite caregiver. As the journal is a familiar item in the environment, sharing it with the respite caregiver is a cue to the individual with dementia. It is a cue of your confidence in the respite caregiver as being safe.

Notes

Chapter 7 - The Supportive Environment in Toileting

Step-by-step organization and cuing in the environment helps simplify and support daily tasks such as toileting. The basic Montessori principles are always the same: *Observe, Standardize,* and *Simplify*. Then provide cues using *Signage*. Together, these principles create support.

"Washroom" and "Bathroom" are both commonly used terms for the room in which we find and use a toilet. Neither of them directly indicate that a toilet is in the room. As the ability to remember weakens, we need first to help individuals with dementia locate the toilet. Just as signage can help identify what is hidden behind a cabinet door, signage can be useful for this in that same way to identify rooms that lie behind a closed door.

Identifying the Toilet Location at Home

Toileting at home is easier than in public spaces because the toilet is always in the same place. The route to it never changes, and there are no new distractions on the way.

But, when you look at the hallways in your home, notice that all the doors look pretty much the same. As the individual with dementia's memory and ability to self-orient deteriorates, this undermines their ability to know which door is hiding the toilet from them.

This is where cuing again comes in. Be forewarned: visitors may be a little puzzled by the cues that they find around the house. They are unlikely to have signs posted in their own homes. However, while the cuing that helps your loved one the most will indeed change the appearance of your home, the decision to put the needs of the individual with dementia first is well worth the trade-off.

We simply identify the room by placing a sign that says "Toilet" on the door. Include both the word and a picture of a toilet if needed. This is extending the practical application of understanding the individual's need for support. By using this signage, you provide a clear identifier as to what is behind the door.

Identifying the Toilet Location in Public Venues

In public spaces, there are many different signs that are intended to let you know where the toilets are located. But, the pictures usually don't include a toilet. The signs also focus on distinguishing between the "Men's Room" and "Ladies' Room." These are two more words commonly used for places where one can use a toilet. Again, these are words that do not identify such rooms as containing a toilet.

Signage like this is based on our common understanding of euphemisms. They use agreed upon pictures that are non-representational symbols. These symbols are used to designate where a toilet is as well as which gender is supposed to use it – two independent pieces of information.

The Montessori Alzheimer's Project

For people without dementia, these are sufficient cues to enable us to identify in which room there is a toilet for us to use. But, the socially agreed upon meanings of those euphemisms and symbols are lost to those who have dementia.

When communicating with an individual who has dementia, euphemisms are simply the wrong way to go. Speak simply and directly. If you ask someone with dementia if they need to use a washroom, you might get back an answer like, *"I don't need to wash."* Or, asking if they need to use the bathroom might produce an answer like, *"I don't need to take a bath."* Those are both correct answers to the direct question, but not to the question clothed in the euphemism.

If you only understand English and are eating in a French restaurant, the sign that says "Hommes" is meaningless to you. You might guess the meaning of "Hommes" when you see "Femmes" in a similar script on a nearby door. You would probably guess correctly by reaching into your memory for a similar pattern ("feminine") and the pattern of signs for men's rooms and ladies' rooms having been seen side-by-side many times in the past. Using that information, you could infer the meaning of "Hommes." This is a valuable kind of analysis to keep in mind for Observation.

For someone with dementia, understanding of the vocabulary and nuances of their own language is progressively weakened. We should not presume that they would be able to reach into their memory for a pattern that would enable them to guess the meaning of a symbol. To presume they can make the leap from a euphemism to its socially agreed upon meaning is a hope that will become progressively less likely to occur as time goes on.

Signage that supports individuals with dementia must be designed based upon their then-current capacities. In that light, consider that an individual with dementia's reaction to a euphemistic image-based sign for a toilet in a public venue is likely to be similar to the reaction that an English-only speaker would have to a sign that says "Hommes," but the person with dementia has lost many of the resources that once would have supported a "translation."

However, a sign with a depiction of a man alongside "Hommes" and a nearby sign saying "Femmes" alongside a depiction of a woman creates one additional cue that allows someone without dementia to make a more informed choice. This same provision would be much more helpful for people with dementia who must deal with signage in their own language. This is another example of how cuing is important for all of us, not just those with dementia.

Image-based signs generally require a secondary analysis to connect the image with the underlying meaning. Let's look at two signs indicating public venue toilets:

Neither of those signs directly communicates that there are toilets behind the door. The first one requires yet another conceptual leap to know that the symbols represent a man and a woman. A further conceptual leap is needed to understand why there would be a gender identification on the door itself. For both, it requires then accessing past patterns to know that they indicate where a toilet is and which gender is to use it.

Understanding the intent of these signs requires an ability to analyze and to understand symbols. This is an ability that may no longer be available to the individual with dementia.

So, adapt communications to the current abilities of individuals with dementia. Don't use euphemisms. Ask the individual directly if they need to use the toilet. Use signage that is clear and which uses images that do not require analysis.

Support Clear Perception

Once the individual with dementia is in the room with the toilet, there is the possibility that they might forget why they are there. Or, they may realize why they are there, but they just can't complete the procedure of actually using the toilet.

These are very real concerns. Many caregivers will quietly tell you that they spend a great deal of time cleaning up toileting accidents inside the bathroom. Their loved one was in the right room, but was unable to take care of themselves effectively. Perhaps they couldn't recall what to do exactly. Perhaps they couldn't recall exactly where to do it – even in that room.

Return again to Observation. Look at the room with your own eyes to imagine how it might appear through the eyes of an individual with dementia.

Most people set up their washroom so that everything matches in a color coordinated way. There is likely:

- A white toilet with a white toilet seat and a white toilet lid.
- The room is often painted a shade of white, with a roll of white toilet paper.
- The floor and any wall tiles are often a shade of white.
- The sink is usually white.
- The hand towel may be white.
- The soap may be white.

The Montessori Alzheimer's Project

A room designed like this might be aesthetically pleasing and visually harmonious. But, it is definitely not a prepared environment that will support an individual with dementia. It provides few cues to guide one to successfully complete the task of toileting.

When everything one sees blends and bleeds together, individual items tend to be harder to see as separate from each other. They can almost disappear in the visual field. This is particularly true for someone whose ability to isolate and discriminate among sense perceptions is not what it used to be.

It is important to prepare and cue the environment to make it easy to identify individual items in the room. This simple preparation will provide cues as to why he/she is in that room. It will also help guide the toileting sequence from commencement to completion.

The large items are the first thing you would likely expect and want to see in this room. This means the toilet and the sink. To help the individual with dementia isolate those items first, paint the wall a color other than a shade of white. This will highlight a white toilet and a white sink, because they will then stand out against the colored background of the wall. Perceptually, their shapes will then become a more easily identified cue standing out in the room.

Next, because we are discussing how the environment can help the individual with dementia organize perceptions, the seat on the toilet should be a different color than the toilet. Not merely white next to off-white, but perhaps a blue seat on a white toilet bowl, so that there is sharp contrast. This makes it far easier to recognize that the toilet seat is up or if it is down.

This is even more important for safety in light of the fact that bones become increasingly brittle as we age. A contrasting-colored toilet seat is much easier to see as the person with dementia is lowering themselves onto it. A broken hip is too often the result of an elderly person, with or without dementia, relaxing their muscles before their bottom touches the toilet seat. They can crash onto the seat, or even the extremely hard porcelain bowl itself, if they don't realize the seat is up rather than down. They run the risk of injuring themselves, purely because they misjudged the height of the seat.

For an individual with dementia, that misjudgment may be due to the fact that the white on white toilet has blurred perceptually with the rest of the room. It may be due to seat being indistinguishable from the bowl itself.

Finally, remove the toilet seat cover, so that only the colored toilet seat itself remains. By removing the toilet seat cover, you further clarify the perceptual field. It is a one-step issue – the seat is up or it is down.

The Sequence of Toileting

Next comes the actual task of toileting. In your home, it unlikely that there are clear cues highlighting exactly what to do in the room. There is no sign showing what to do where, in what order, and how to do it. While there is no need for this in a home without someone with dementia, for caregiving at home this can be critical.

When we are young, toileting is learned by slowly and repeatedly reviewing each step of the task in sequence. It begins with asking a child if they need to use the toilet. This guides them to connect a specific sensation in their body to the next step of thinking about using the toilet. We then teach them to lift the toilet lid and to raise/lower the seat as needed.

We continue by guiding the child to pull down their pants, underclothes, and then to sit on the toilet. After they have completed their toileting, we teach them to wash and then dry their hands. Done enough times, this becomes second nature – an automatic sequence of remembered steps – and in that way, muscle memory is engaged.

For the individual with dementia, the automatic sequence is no longer so automatic. It is no longer second nature. Through cues and by triggering muscle memory, the sequence can become accessible.

For those without dementia, the routine is so ingrained that it no longer seems like a task with sequential steps. We don't really have to think about what to do, in what order, etc. We simply go into the bathroom, use the toilet, wash our hands, and leave. But in fact, it is a sequence. We have just internalized it so that it is accessed when we experience that familiar body sensation.

Toileting is a task for all of us, every day. It sounds pretty simple because, for most of us, it is. This is not the case, however, for a person with dementia.

Having broken down the sequence one uses for the task of toileting, the next step is to provide cues. Yes, this may mean putting a detailed, illustrated poster or a set of cue cards up on the wall by the toilet. And yes, it shows every person who enters the room the many steps that they must take to use the toilet properly.

Having a poster or set of cue cards is probably not your concept of a stylish bathroom. It is definitely not the original look you were going for. But style is not relevant to an individual with dementia unless it addresses their needs

What is important is functionality, pathways to succeed at tasks, and minimizing obstacles to achievement. Posting these instructions will actually liberate you from much of the hope and fear that becomes associated with toileting an individual with dementia.

The goal here is for the new and modified environment to support the then-current abilities of the individual with dementia. And remember, every successful toileting event becomes a positive experience for both the individual and the caregiver.

The environment now eliminates confusion. It protects your loved one from a sense of shame when accidents happen. That eliminates the need for the caregiver to deal with the negative emotional impact of toileting accidents. Just eliminating some toileting cleanups, if not most or all, makes life easier and more tranquil in the home.

Posting a step-by-step series of cue cards on the wall by the toilet helps the individual with dementia to complete the toileting process in the right sequence.[5]

The second to the last illustrated cue in the toileting sequence is for pulling up one's clothes when finished. Then, to identify what comes next, there is a final cue in the sequence directing the individual to the next task. The illustration should direct them to the sink, and at the sink there is a new set of cues for washing their hands.

Remember that transitions are often where an individual with dementia becomes panicked as the question of "what next?" occurs. The linkage between the cue cards by the toilet with the cue cards by the sink assists the individual with dementia to make that transition. The cued signage leads from using the toilet to washing the hands afterwards. That keeps it simple.

The transition is supported so as to support self-direction in the transition. The separate cue cards at the sink are there for the task of handwashing. They stand on their own when handwashing is needed, separate and apart from toileting.

For every task, break down the activity into its "bite-sized" components, with cues leading to each next step. When

---

[5] Links to cues for toileting and handwashing can be found at: www.montessorialzheimersproject.com

transitions are needed at the end of a task, include guidance for that transition as the last cue. This supports the existing capacities of the individual with dementia as well as emphasizing and reinforcing the muscle memory that is part of the cued task.

We can re-engage muscle memory in toileting as well as in washing hands by cues and repetition. Successfully triggering muscle memory smooths the transitions between the cued step-by-step instructions. Every successful transition generates confidence and self-esteem within that task.

Toileting Away from Home

As we discussed, journaling enables you to more accurately predict the general timing of toileting in any given day. Keeping in mind that walks and other longer trips will likely require toileting away from home, consider how to establish a supportive environment for toileting outside the home. Public facilities are unlikely to have cued support guidance. So, let's go back to our task of Observation.

In a public space or in another family's home, there are no highlighted cues for what to do in the toilet. There are no cues because most of us have used the toilet alone without cues since we were young. With forethought, we can develop options to use in these situations.

The Montessori Alzheimer's Project

Prepare for this likely event ahead of time. This is because familiarization, practice, and regular routines are incredibly helpful supports to include in all tasks. At home, which is the safest place, begin to re-introduce the experience of having the caregiver accompany the individual with dementia into the toileting room. They can give the necessary verbal cues and then stand immediately outside the door.

This is how we learned how to use the toilet when we were young. We don't need to treat the individual with dementia as if they never learned how to use the toilet in the past. Rather, being there to provide cues is how we can support the task under the current circumstances of dementia.

In this way, when toileting is required outside the home, there is already some familiarity with having someone right there to help with simple direct verbal cues as necessary. By establishing this routine at home, you can appropriately project normalcy to the individual with dementia when toileting outside the home.

Practice this by including your presence, physically and/or verbally when toileting in your own home. Familiarizing the individual with dementia to a new pattern is the foundation that creates a sense of ordinary ease, of normalcy, rather than a sense of tension. Then, if you are in someone else's home or a public venue, this is already the familiar routine. There is now a similarity to the way things customarily happen at home.

Go into the washroom together without doubt or hesitation. That is the cue of safety, of inviting trust in the environment. In your home, provide the verbal cues that match the posted picture and text clues. Depending on the comfort of the individual with dementia, state that you will stay right outside the door to help as needed. If it is more appropriate, given their present abilities, for you to stay in the washroom, simply turning away can give a sense of privacy that further projects ordinariness and normalcy.

If you do exit the room to wait outside, state that out loud, saying, *"I am right outside in case you need me."* Continue verbally cuing each step of the process as needed, guiding the sequence through the final handwashing steps. This means following the same step-by-step breakdown of the toileting task as is posted in your home toileting room. Mentally rehearse the actions that you will take if the individual with dementia goes into a public washroom and forgets why he is there. Know ahead of time what you are going to do and say if this happens. Just letting him know that you are there is the most important cue of safety you can provide. In public facilities, use the handicapped washroom so that there is no issue of a caregiver entering a facility set up for the opposite gender.

The daily routine of toileting in your home is the foundation for support when using the toilet outside the home environment. Your voice becomes the substitute for the cue cards. This is another way to extend the safe and stable environment at home to the outside experience.

The trade-off for the caregiver is likely to be limited to some questioning looks from passers-by in a mall, or from friends with whom you're visiting. Just keep the explanation ordinary and simple, such as *"This is helpful to him so now it is how we do it."* That is a small price to pay for avoiding catastrophic reactions outside the home, and their consequences.

Notes

Chapter 8 – Redirection

A prepared environment enables caregivers to reduce the number of difficulties that confront an individual with dementia. Preparation of your home environment as MAP recommends creates tools that can be brought to bear as needed. But even in a prepared environment, unanticipated issues will arise.

Sometimes, the prepared environment needs to be adjusted on the spot to shift an unsafe or difficult situation for an individual with dementia to something safe or easy. The answer to this need is another foundational Montessori principle: Redirection.

The technique of Redirection can make a big difference in the day-to-day lives of individuals with dementia and their caregivers. With Redirection, caregivers have an immediate positive impact on the individual with dementia. This positive impact avoids much of the stress in caregiving is incredibly rewarding feedback for the caregiver.

It is important to observe and to analyze, as always, so that the caregiver can accomplish those specific goals of safety and ease. Caregivers need to avoid setting up a confrontation, but at the same time they have to protect the individual with dementia by eliminating danger.

Working with the information we gather through Observation, we can analyze context – the causes and conditions around the triggering difficulty. With that information identified, we can address the negative momentum of the individual with dementia by applying Redirection.

Redirection in the Real World

The MAP approach is concerned with real world issues that caregivers face every day. Redirection means shifting the momentum of a situation, rather than having a head-on confrontation with it. The individual with dementia is redirected, meaning that they are led to a different focal point that is safe.

Here is an example of redirection at work:

At a certain point in the progression of his Alzheimer's Disease, my father was no longer capable of driving safely. For everyone's well-being, a person with dementia should not drive under these circumstances. My mother was unable to figure out how to stop him from driving. She was equally unable to see how she might put a decision to prevent him from driving into action. She was frightened of his likely reaction, which may well have been expressions of anger.

If this issue confronts you, as it did me, you firstly have to decide whether or not it is safe for the individual with dementia to drive. You can certainly check with your doctor, but the doctor is unlikely to have had the direct experience of being a passenger in a car driven by the individual with dementia. So, you may not get a firm, cut and dried answer there.

The Montessori Alzheimer's Project

Here is a simpler method that you can use. Just ask yourself: *"Would I allow my child to be driven by the person with dementia whose driving ability I have come to doubt?"*

If there is even a moment of hesitation in answering that question, then the answer is crystal clear. It is *no*. It is no longer safe for this person to drive himself, or anyone else. The answer is based upon your gut level intuition. No medical tests are needed.

When my father displayed a failing ability to drive, my mother was quite frightened, but she was emotionally incapable of taking his car keys and license away. She was afraid of destroying his self-esteem. She was equally afraid of triggering a huge fight with him, of triggering a catastrophic reaction.

My father had always been the driver when they went anywhere in the car together. But she had already started to shift that habit to a new routine where she was happily becoming his chauffeur. However, he still would get into the car sometimes and drive them to somewhere close by or he would get into the car and drive by himself.

One day, he stopped in the middle of an intersection. He stopped because he couldn't remember whether he was supposed to turn right, turn left, or go straight ahead. That was when she called me, telling me she was afraid of his driving. She also said that she couldn't deal with taking his driver's license away.

I flew to visit them a few days later, as quickly as I could arrange it. I arrived at their house and, before going inside, I removed the distributor cap from my father's car. That disabled his car. Later that day, my father wanted to drive somewhere. We went outside together, but the car wouldn't start. He told me that there was something wrong with the car. I agreed, saying that we would have to have someone look at it.

In simple terms, I had modified the driving environment. I had, in Montessori terms, quietly and unobtrusively prepared the environment for safety. In this case, it was safety for my father and everyone else that might share the road with him, including those driving their own cars, riding a bicycle on the street, or walking on an adjacent sidewalk.

That is not the end of the story. I modified the environment successfully for safety but, remember, we want to avoid catastrophic reactions. This usually means avoiding a conflict and any resulting confrontation.

Having adjusted the environment of the car, and having told him that we'd have to have someone look into why it wouldn't start, I redirected my father's attention. I immediately invited him for a walk. I pointed out the beautiful sky, the flowers, and so on. I simply said: *"Well we aren't driving anywhere right now because the car isn't working, so let's take a walk and see what's happening in the neighborhood."*

The result of this redirection was the warm interaction of walking together outside on a beautiful sunny day. It involved physical activity that grounded him in movement. It took him physically away from the object that triggered the safety issue. There was no panic attack, no catastrophic reaction, and no problem. Instead, the redirection was itself a transition to safety and ease.

We had the same conversation about the car that would not start each of the next few days. Each day I agreed with him that we would have to get someone to look at it and then we went for a walk. My father simply stopped asking about the car by day four. A few days later, I removed the car from the driveway. According to my mother's wishes, it was given to my sister, who lived on the other side of the country.

My father never asked about the car again, and never drove any car after that. He was already accustomed to sitting in the passenger seat of my mother's car. There was no further transition needed because sitting in that passenger seat was a reliable, known spot for him.

This anecdote illustrates use of the Montessori principles of the prepared environment, and of redirection. Here, they were being applied far from a preschool classroom. Those same principles were used to avoid danger, to avoid conflict, and to invite warmth.

To summarize the intervention for safety:

- First, there was the preparation/appropriate adjustment of the environment.

- Then, there was the simple agreement of the facts – the acknowledgment that yes, something was wrong with the car.
- Finally, the attention was redirected elsewhere to something inviting that involved physical movement away from the object at issue – the car.

This approach simply bypasses the conceptual difficulties of the patient. It lowers, and indeed can eliminate, the risk of confrontation. It can avoid even the need to explain what you have done to prepare the environment. At its best, there is no criticism and no power struggle.

With confrontation, the likelihood is that the caregiver will end up trying to argue logically with someone to whom logic is no longer accessible. Arguing logically with an individual with dementia is never going to be successful. The redirection here eliminated the very real possibility of a car accident involving my father, others in the car, pedestrians, and others on the road.

Proactive Redirection

The approach of disabling a distributor cap will not work in all cases. Sometimes the person with dementia will become extremely angry if they cannot drive, or if you are preventing them from doing something else. This possibility may be minimized by creating a change in habit before the change is necessary.

In this case, my mother had begun implementing a change by taking on a new role of chauffeur. She volunteered to drive whenever driving somewhere was required. It usually worked. But, in the end, she needed some additional support, as most every caregiver does, to take that last difficult step.

Anticipate future issues such as this. Then, structure present approaches to prepare for and perhaps even to eliminate the future issue. Just like using name tags before they are absolutely necessary, one makes the shift slowly and gently. Think of it like this: Whatever the approaching issue might be, structure the environment and what happens in it <u>now</u>, so that you "become the chauffeur" before a confrontation about the issue is unavoidable.

The approach is to identify future issues and to install new habits and patterns before the dangers of these future issues become overwhelmingly evident.

Here is a less dramatic example, where early redirection engendered warmth and further trust.

My father liked to play golf. During one visit a few years after his diagnosis, he decided he wanted us to play a round of golf together. Everything went well for the first few holes. A nice walk, a few swings, a few laughs. By the time we reached the 5th hole, things started to shift.

He lined up at the tee, standing correctly between the markers that indicate where to tee off. But, he was facing exactly the wrong direction. By force of habit, he was standing in the correct spot. By force of muscle memory, he was in the correct posture for teeing off. However, he was aiming 180 degrees in the wrong direction.

I asked him gently if he was feeling tired. He said, *"Yes."* I said, *"Then let's just go home."*

He looked at me to see if he had done something wrong. Then he asked if it was really OK to just leave. I said: *"Sure! We've had a nice time on the golf course and now we can go have a nice time at home."*

He immediately relaxed, trusting my words and body language. We walked off the course with my arm around his shoulders. He had the physical contact of my arm around his shoulders guiding him. My words expressed warmth both in tone and content. And why not? There was no concern but to enjoy the walk home.

This is an example of making the person with dementia feel safe when they are becoming (or are likely to become) stressed. Act as soon as you see that this might happen, by gently suggesting a change of activity, in whatever way suggests itself by the circumstances. Then, the next step of redirecting their attention toward further ease and safety is initiated. Once again, the redirection involved physical movement away from the triggering difficulty.

Redirection Toward Equilibrium

Maintaining the equilibrium of the individual with dementia is always paramount. That equilibrium can be upset by external circumstances as well as by things going on inside him. It can also be upset by well-meant attempts to explain to or reason with the person with dementia.

The Montessori Alzheimer's Project

Some people may hear these stories and feel that a lie was being told. They may feel that there is something inherently wrong with what they would characterize as a level of deception. While this may be one way of looking at the incident, consider the potential alternative: a catastrophic reaction.

Sometimes we make the decision to say things that are not exactly true or to avoid saying things, in order to spare the individual with dementia from unsuccessful confrontations with their growing limitations. We need to protect them from difficulties that will, without protection, likely lead to them cascading down into an emotional collapse. While the content, the words, may not be exactly true – after all, I knew that I had disabled the car – the emotional content of protecting this person that I loved, was absolutely authentic and heartfelt.

The decision to take any particular approach is a personal one based upon one's own beliefs, based upon the circumstances, based upon one's Observations, and based upon one's knowledge of the person with dementia. Each caregiver must decide in advance whether or not he or she is willing to prepare the environment for the person with dementia in such a way, and then to guide the interactions that arise.

The difficulties associated with adjusting the environment need to be weighed in terms of both the direct, immediate benefit to the person with dementia, and the overall benefit of avoiding catastrophic reactions that will likely occur if action is not taken to support that person.

Notes

The Montessori Alzheimer's Project

Chapter 9 - Cuing for Visitors

For both caregivers and people with dementia, visitors can be a welcome addition to the daily routine. But, they can also be triggers for panic, discomfort, and fear. One of the goals of MAP is to reduce/eliminate those negative emotions in both people with dementia and in their caregivers. At the same time, MAP seeks to eliminate negatives that visitors may experience. Let's look at how cues in the environment can address these concerns.

Preparing Adult Visitors

Visitors may include old friends, relatives (close and distant), nurses, and respite caregivers. They will become a part of the home environment the moment they arrive, so some pre-visit preparation is helpful. Then, they enter more seamlessly into the prepared home environment.

For visitors who have not been in the home since it was modified according to MAP principles, a simple *Visitor's Guide* can be helpful. The intent is to provide a background, some explanation of the changes that they'll encounter, so as to maximize the positive interactions visitors can have when engaging the individual with dementia. This approach also reduces the possibility of a visitor unintentionally triggering a negative interaction.

Before visitors arrive, on one of the days leading up to the visit, share with them your *Visitor's Guide* so that they will arrive prepared. What follows is the MAP Visitor's Guide form.[6] It is short and includes the kinds of things you may wish to include in your own personalized guide.

Montessori Alzheimer's Project Visitor's Guide

Welcome To Our Home!

Our home may look a bit different than it used to. As you know, _____ is in the early stages of dementia. So, we have changed our home to make our time with _him/her_ joyful and warm. By making these changes in our house, we can support _____ 's ability to stay here with us for as long as possible, happy and safe. We want to enable him to share good memories with us, and to create new ones together.

Please wear a name tag. _____ may not need it, but it is always helpful. It eliminates any embarrassment if _he/she_ can't recall your name when _he/she_ first sees you. Please also introduce yourself each time with a smile, say your name and your relationship to _____. A simple: "Hi ____, it's ____, your son." This makes for a great start to the visit.

You will notice a variety of cues in the house. There are, for example, pictures of what is in a cabinet or behind a door. With these cues, _____ has the support _he/she_ needs to

---

[6] This is available in multiple languages at www.montessorialzheimersproject.com

The Montessori Alzheimer's Project

stay here at home with us safely and as a valued contributor to the day-to-day life of the household.

Tasks and Games are great things to do together. Here is a list of some of the things that you and _____ might want to do together during your visit:

> *a)*
>
> *b)*
>
> *c)*
>
> *d)*

Of course, just sitting holding hands, talking, listening to music, or walking together is wonderful too.

We have a material from the Montessori Alzheimer's Project *and* The Alzheimer's Family Manual *that you can always look through. It has tips for how to walk with _____, and how to talk, play, sing and do all kinds of things together with _____.*

While things aren't quite the same as they were, they don't have to be all that different. Loving kindness will overcome almost anything.

Don't hesitate to ask me for suggestions to make your visits special for both _____ and you.

Again, welcome to our home.

In this way, from the very beginning, we create a foundation for the visitor to understand the changes that have been made in the environment. Having already received an explanation of this approach, visitors enter the space and can begin their interactions with the individual with dementia, already prepared. They are already aware of the importance of paying attention to the existing cues in the environment, and to the importance of interactive cues that support the person with dementia.

Encourage regular visitors to wear predictable outfits with not too much variety. For example, if someone typically wore a hat or blue jeans when they visited in the past, they should take care to continue to do this when they visit. When visitors standardize their appearance, they remain more easily recognizable for the person with dementia.

Asking them to introduce themselves in a simple, ordinary way each time they arrive is extremely important. Too often, when people visit individuals with dementia, they begin their greeting with a test, as we have discussed. This is not done with bad intent. They want to find out what he remembers, or what he fails to remember.

We are forewarning them to avoid this. Instead, visitors should be cued to use a stock greeting: *"Hi Jerry, it is your friend Lenny. I am back to visit again. It is great to see you."* In that way, you are guiding them to participate in cuing of the person with dementia.

Institute these changes before they become necessary. Simple cues like this promote relaxation with the visitor, rather than a stress response to uncertainty. There will more likely be a smile of recognition on the face of the person with dementia.

The positive interactions that take place within the support of such cues will more than repay everyone's efforts in taking these steps. With encouragement, visitors can participate in this even to the extent of wearing the same (freshly laundered) outfit that they wore for their last visit.

The idea is to make your home space as comfortable as possible for everyone that is part of the visit. If in doubt, make any decision in favor of the comfort of the individual with dementia. It is best to start from the very beginning to set him at ease. That sets up an environment of comfort that can be extended into the social interactions that will happen during the visit.

If visitors are given guidance from the beginning, they will feel more comfortable engaging the person with dementia as they enter the modified space. They will not be confused by your home looking different than it did before. Instead, they likely will feel welcomed as a participant in warmth and kindness. They will not feel compelled to ask questions about the signage you may have put up. The *Visitor's Guide* will enable visitors to appreciate that all of this is done for the person with dementia, with deep love and respect.

One important aspect of comfort for visitors is to provide suggestions on what they might do while they are visiting. Again, look to the foundation of cuing. For old friends or family, telling stories to the person with dementia, of events from their lives together, can be warm and touching. For most people with dementia, old memories are far more accessible than new ones, so use that to guide you. Family pictures in an album can be used as a very warm point of engagement to start the process of sharing these stories. The photos that are displayed as the stories are told function as another cuing reference for the person with dementia.

Putting on favorite music from the past can also trigger positive engagement. It can trigger old memories, lead to singing and even to dancing. Having a "Playlist of Your Life" that visitors can use often serves as a wonderful adjunct to any visit.

Encouraging walks together, with the instructions on how to walk beside a person with dementia is another way to create warm space and movement.[7] This can ease visitors' occasional discomfort with the silences that may take place during visits. Pointing out things in the garden, looking at indoor plants, and talking perhaps about pets are all positive focal points. Provide particular topics for the visitors to talk about with their loved one, topics that you have noted in your journal as positive.

Preparing Young Children

Preparation for young visitors, such as grandchildren, is at least as important as preparing adults. Those visits can have wonderful impacts on the individual with dementia. As

---

[7] Guidance on walking together is found at www.montessorialzheimersproject.com

always, preparation can eliminate many potential difficulties for everyone.

Again, keep things simple and direct. Just letting a child know that Grandpa may forget more things these days – including their names – prepares them for that likely occurrence. Simultaneously, assure them that this doesn't change Grandpa's love for them, just as it doesn't change for anyone else whose name he might forget.

Let them know that Grandpa may ask the same question a few times, even if they have already answered him. Tell them that this is OK, and that it is fine to just answer it again with a smile.

If the person with dementia has occasional outbursts, warn the children gently in advance that if Grandpa starts looking frustrated or seems to be getting upset, it is good to offer him some water, or to hold his hand and smile. It is important for other adults to be close at hand, to intervene as necessary. They can be there to redirect the individual with dementia should there be frustration or upset. The goal is to avoid the potential catastrophic reaction. This ensures that both the children and the individual with dementia are able to have a positive experience free from fear. Avoiding those difficulties will make it easier for children to return for more visits.

Prepare the environment so there are activities that children can do together with the person with dementia. These activities might include drawing together or playing simple card games within their respective capacities. Create opportunities for grandchildren to have positive memories of the person with dementia. It will have tremendous benefit for many years in the future for those children, while bringing joy to the parents and grandparents involved.

This is Montessori's principle of preparing the environment, this time applied to the arrival of visitors. Prepared visitors enrich and complement the already physically prepared environment. This will benefit the person with dementia, the visitors, and the caregiver.

When visitors understand how they are being welcomed as well as how to work with and within the cued environment, their visits are prepared to be more joyful and soothing to the heart. This can lead to more frequent visits. The result is more social support for both the individual with dementia and the caregiver. In addition, it can open the door to visitors who to consider joining the respite care team.

Notes

Chapter 10 - Caring for the Caregiver

The last topic for this introduction to the Montessori Alzheimer's Project is the issue of caring for the caregiver. Protecting the well-being of caregivers is key to protecting the well-being of the individuals with dementia. In the MAP program, caring for caregivers is another opportunity to Observe, Standardize, Simplify and use Signage to modify the everyday environment of the caregiving experience.

Without a trained, loving, and compassionate caregiver, the individual with dementia will continue to encounter increasingly difficult obstacles to daily life. The individual with dementia is losing the ability to self-regulate his interactions with the environment and with others in his world. In other words, life is heading towards ongoing and frightening stress without relief. The primary caregiver provides measured regulation in the life of the individual with dementia, which becomes indispensable to that person's well-being.

Primary caregivers tend to be the person interfacing directly with the world on behalf of individuals with dementia. This transition takes place as those individuals increasingly have difficulty doing it themselves. It is the primary caregiver who is best positioned to understand the need to adjust the environment for the benefit of the individual with dementia. They are also the best positioned to understand that adjusting the environment to match the then-current abilities of individual with dementia shift on an ongoing basis will continue to provide benefit.

Meeting the Needs of the Caregiver

The focus of the MAP program is on adjusting the environment to support the individual with dementia. While these environmental adjustments are for the benefit of the individual with dementia, it must be remembered that the caregiver is a key part of that environment. In many ways, those same adjustments also support the caregiver, and there are some adjustments to consider that are specific to the caregivers' needs. Firstly, let's examine this idea that preparing the environment for a person with dementia also benefits the caregiver. What are some examples of this?

One critical benefit is that a supportive, prepared environment tends to reduce the number of catastrophic reactions that occur. As a result, the primary caregiver experiences less of those tremendously stressful events. This enables the caregiver to conserve energy that would otherwise be needed to manage them, which tends to lower the caregiver's personal stress. The result is that the caregiver is able to more consistently interact and nurture in the context of dementia.

Another benefit is that these environmental adjustments directly support the caregiver's needs. A simplified supportive, prepared environment makes it easier for respite caregivers to smoothly enter the caregiving environment. The more easily accessible the adjusted environment is for respite care workers, the better they can provide continuity in caring for the individual with dementia. The better they can provide respite care, the more easily primary caregivers can feel free to take a break This is true for short as well as more extended breaks from being the onsite primary caregiver.

Feelings of Being Overwhelmed

Being a long-term caregiver is stressful. It takes a lot to always focus one's energy on another individual. But without any break to take care of one's own needs, it can become overwhelming. This simply doesn't work on any long-term basis.

By applying Standardization and Simplifying to the caregiving tasks, the world becomes less overwhelming for the caregiver. By using Signage, caregivers provide further environmental support. These techniques all bring more of a sense of workability to the caregiving experience. Then, with Observation, we can consider modifying the environment so as to provide space to meet the personal needs of the caregiver, for the well-being of the caregiver.

In the earlier chapter about modifying the kitchen cabinets, we discussed the benefit of eliminating as many items as possible from the environment. That benefit was focused on the needs of the individual with dementia. For the caregiver, this may be a difficult change, an indication that she is losing control of her own life. It can be very difficult to give up even more autonomy, even more control of the environment because the following questions can arise, *"What about me? Where am I in all this?"*

So, for you as the caregiver, set aside a space where those things precious to you can be kept. Label that space with your name as a cue that your beloved items are kept there, not the household utensils. That is Signage. Use the walls in the house to hang photos and art that makes you happy.

Standardize the walls as part of your space. Only use the walls to hold meaningful items that work as cues such as photos. Photos, which can be easily put into a rotation, encourage good memories, conversation and the sharing of stories. Simplify means to leave lots of space on the walls so that the photos stand out from each other. Rotating photos allows you to refresh the environment without adversely impacting the support it provides. Your ability to use the environment in this way can nourish you and remind you that your place in the world is not limited to caregiving.

Feelings of Guilt

Another common caregiver experience is feeling guilty about that experience of being overwhelmed. Feeling guilty about not being the perfect caregiver is an emotion common to most, if not all, caregivers at some point. We are human. We are subject to the ordinary human emotions that arise during the long-term task of caring for another human being subject to dementia.

Primary caregivers often find that feelings of guilt sometimes surge uncontrollably into their consciousness. This depletes their energy even further. Sometimes it is guilt about events long past, events that took place prior to the onset of dementia.

It is true that even though those events are long past, a sense of guilt can arise. You might feel that you should apologize in some way for past deeds that may, appropriately or not, trigger that sense of guilt in you. Caregiving with kindness is how you can embody that apology directly and without embarrassment.

Sometimes caregivers feel guilty about taking time for themselves. When you utilize journals as recommended by the MAP program, you will likely come to understand the importance of recharging your own batteries. This can happen as you identify the changes in the environment that trigger difficulties, and the changes that put everyone in the environment at ease.

A study of your journal entries will likely highlight how things function when you are tired compared with how things function when you are rested. Usually, the depth of one's patience – a foundation of being kind – changes based on how rested you are.

Paying attention to your own needs, recharging your own batteries, supports your caregiving as you want it to be. As a result, inappropriate feelings of guilt will tend to become progressively weakened – as they should be. Ultimately, when you actually experience the benefits of respite care for yourself, such thoughts will start to become like any other. In other words, they can be experienced as just another passing thought and therefore no big deal.

The Importance of Respite Care

The use of respite caregivers is vital in meeting the needs of the caregiver. Respite caregivers allow primary caregivers to take the time and space necessary for themselves, while at the same time ensuring continuity of care. The use of journals, as discussed in earlier chapters, enables the primary caregiver to take those breaks knowing that the critical information needed for each day's pattern is right at hand for the respite caregiver's use and guidance.

Respite care enables you, the primary caregiver, to maintain your ability to continue to be a caregiver. You need a break. If you are weary, if you are feeling overwhelmed, please understand that this is absolutely the most common experience of primary caregivers. Taking time, taking respite for yourself, is the medicine you need. It is the space to discharge and recharge.

Introducing the Respite Caregiver

It is important to gently introduce the respite caregiver into the environment. Take the time to familiarize the individual with dementia and the respite caregiver with one another. The first time or two (or even three) that you have respite care at the home, don't leave. Have a cup of tea while the respite care person slowly transitions into the caregiver role, on-site. Your relaxation models the behavior you want the respite caregiver to display. It is a cue for the individual with dementia to recognize the respite caregiver as safe.

Make sure that you demonstrate your comfort with, and confidence in, the respite caregiver. Do this clearly in the presence of the individual with dementia. Encourage the respite caregiver the engage with you first. If they try to immediately connect to the individual with dementia, it will be likely viewed with suspicion. Sit together and use the journal to help them become familiar with the routine and the schedule.

Allow for the gradual extension of warmth you project to go beyond the individual with dementia so as to include the respite caregiver. This is key to avoiding, or at least diminishing, any fears that might arise in connection with the respite caregiver entering the home.

The more the respite caregiver is perceived as an ordinary part of the environment, the simpler the transition is. In that way, when you do leave the home for your break, it is less likely that your departure will trigger a fear of abandonment. Both you and the individual with dementia are more likely to have a positive experience. This is how to build the foundation of a respite caregiver relationship in the environment.

Support Groups

As most people know from experience, simply telling yourself that your emotions aren't rational isn't so helpful. It doesn't eliminate the power of those emotions. We do know that one thing does help. Based on the experiences of caregiver support groups of every variety, sharing one's feelings within the safety of a support group can be helpful.

Consider the environment of a support group from your point of view, just as we consider environments for the individual with dementia. Is the environment helpful or is it an obstacle?

Support groups, in name and function, are designed to be a safe space for you to share with others on that same journey. It is an intentionally created environment filled with other people who have dealt with, and who are currently dealing with, these same experiences and emotions.

Support groups provide the warmth of an understanding and generally quite non-judgmental community. You might find that you are judging yourself far more harshly than others (who are experiencing similar circumstances) judge you. That alone can help you release some of the negative energy you might hold onto tightly because you are seeing yourself as less than a perfect caregiver.

Support groups allow you to express as well as to release those emotions. The feedback that the group provides can help to validate your own experience. Participants offer supportive responses, personal insights, and very often truly helpful advice – all of which comes from others on a similar journey to your own.

Some people may feel embarrassed or uncomfortable at the thought of exposing their need for support. They tend to avoid caregiver support groups for just this reason. They seem to feel that admitting a need for support means that they are admitting that they are inadequate to the task, that they are failing as a caregiver. This is not so different from the individual with dementia being embarrassed or uncomfortable as they sense their own growing inadequacies.

It is OK, of course, to feel that way. Again, this is not uncommon. But please visit one or more support groups and just listen. Check out the environment. Look to see if it might meet your needs.
There is no obligation to speak in these groups. You don't have to say anything to actually get support; just being in that environment is helpful. The warmth will be there whether you choose to speak or not. Just hearing others speak of their own difficulties and emotions can provide reassurance that you are not alone. It shows you that there is a path, and that there are others willing to share their experience on that same path and to support you on your own journey.

Some people may be embarrassed or uncomfortable at the prospect of speaking with friends about the trials and tribulations of being a caregiver. You may be surprised at how many of your friends have had their own experiences dealing with family members and friends with dementia. Perhaps they have experienced caregiving for individuals with illnesses other than dementia. They may be able and willing to provide the direct support that you need, and have only been waiting for you to ask.

So, try putting a toe in that particular water as well. You may find that your friends are more than willing to listen. They may even be willing to accompany you to a support group meeting. That is another way to ease your concerns about participating in one.

Having a friend accompanying you is an extension of the guidance that suggests changing your environment to one of deeper support based on your personal needs as a caregiver. You may feel safer when you go along with a trusted friend for the first meeting or two, until you get to know the other participants.

<u>Use the Respite Care for Your Needs</u>

Primary caregivers who have the opportunity to take respite care breaks often see respite as something other than a chance to have a break. Instead, they see it as a chance to take care of all the mundane daily or weekly tasks they have put off while caregiving. We strongly encourage you to work with those tasks as part of the adjusted everyday environment of caregiving rather than using respite care time. Why? It is because *the respite time is for you.*

Observe yourself: what is it that you think about doing when you have respite coverage? Do you view respite coverage as an opportunity to take care of household bookkeeping or other tasks you have been putting off? We encourage you instead to view it as a chance to give yourself some breathing space, some warmth.

Respite time is <u>your</u> time to recharge, to connect with friends, to participate in support groups, to go to a movie, maybe to read a book or to walk with friends. It is time for you to do whatever eases your mind and replenishes your energies. Perhaps just being alone for a while with no obligation to engage with anyone might be truly helpful. Please use your respite time for what you need.

Take that time to be "off-duty." Being off-duty can be wonderful, so long as you use it to give you what you need. And what you need, when caregiving is coming closer and closer to overwhelming you, is a temporary break. Don't wait until you are overwhelmed, and don't simply fill that time up with more tasks.
There is life outside caregiving. There will be life after caregiving. So connect with that greater sense of life. In the case of family members, connect with what is going on in their lives, or perhaps in the lives of their children. This ordinary kind of chatting cuts down on the sense of isolation that often afflicts caregivers. It gives you the direct experience that you are part of a larger world to engage with, to learn from, to share with, and to be nourished by.

Maintaining connections with the world outside your caregiving is a positive thing to do. Use the connections to support your own health because that will actually enhance your caregiving abilities. Open that door, that window of opportunity. It can ventilate an environment that has a tendency to become claustrophobic.

Some caregivers think that the proof of their love for the individual with dementia is measured by how long they can manage caregiving alone. That is simply a mistaken view. Caregiving for individuals with dementia is a long-term proposition. Taking care of yourself is the best way to ensure that you are there for them, and will continue to be there for them long-term. With the benefits of respite care in mind, schedule it before you feel overwhelmed.

Caregiving is not a contest. It is not a challenge to see how much you can take before you break. It is about making sure that you remain healthy so that you can provide the best possible caregiving for someone you love. If you are healthy, it is much easier to remain stable, patient, and kind so as to be the caregiver you wish to be.

Just as marathon runners pace themselves to ensure they are able to complete the run, caregivers need to pace themselves. In the marathon that can be caregiving, pacing oneself means scheduling and using respite care.

You are indispensable, the key part of your loved one's environment, so take care of yourself. Always remember that caring for yourself is of direct benefit to the individual with dementia. Without you, life will no doubt be much more difficult for him.

Notes

AFTERWORD

We hope you found the material presented in this introduction to the Montessori Alzheimer's Project to be of benefit. While we cannot eliminate dementia through the use of Montessori principles, we are confident that these principles will make life for those with dementia, and for those caring for them, gentler, safer, and filled with consistent warmth. We believe they are the foundation for staying sane and loving during the difficult parts of the caregiving journey.

Dementia impacts people regardless of race, gender, class, or financial resources. The Montessori Alzheimer's Project is dedicated to helping all people impacted by dementia so that they can have better lives and a journey that avoids some of the known, difficult obstacles.

It is our wish that the love which is the heart of caregiving will be nourished by the ever deeper connections caregivers make with each other and with their loved ones.

With best wishes on your journey,

The Montessori Alzheimer's Project

www.ingramcontent.com/pod-product-compliance
Lightning Source LLC
Chambersburg PA
CBHW051653040426
42446CB00009B/1109